CONTENTS

KU-470-103

Introduction

As domestic birds, canaries hold a position midway between those such as poultry and pigeons, which have been associated with man for many centuries, and others, like the Budgerigar or Zebra Finch, which are of relatively recent introduction. It was first mentioned in a work on natural history in the middle years of the sixteenth century. The writer, Conrad Gesner, had evidently not yet seen a specimen for, having just finished describing the citril, he added, 'Similar to this, so I hear, is a bird of sweetest song called the canary which is brought from the Canary Islands'.

The earliest attempts at domesticating the bird seems to have taken place in Italy. There is a story, often quoted in many of the earlier books on the subject, of a ship carrying a consignment of canaries to Leghorn, which was wrecked off the Isle of Elba. The canaries escaped and evidently found the habitat so suitable to their needs that they settled down and soon established a thriving colony which survived for a number of years.

More positive proof of their being first domesticated in Italy comes from the writer Olina. In 1622 he stated that canaries were being successfully bred in captivity and that there was even sufficient surplus for some to be exported to Germany.

During the seventeenth century canaries appear to have spread throughout western Europe and eventually into Britain, traditionally introduced by the Flemish refugees from across the English Channel. By 1675 they were described by Josiah Blagrove as being bred in England although not on the same scale as in Germany and Italy.

As a result of the artificial conditions imposed upon the birds by domestication, departures from the wild type of plumage began to occur. First, probably, the occasional white feather or two appeared in the wings and tail, and then an entire white tail or several white flights in the wings. Later, light feathers appeared on other parts of the body and the plumage began to break up into pied or broken areas. Such patterns occur in many species of domestic animals.

A complete list of these early variations was given in an old French work on canaries. It also mentioned the completely clear yellow bird which was rarest at that time. All of these plumage variations are still to be found in most breeds of canary to this day and often form the basis for classification at the shows.

During the eighteenth century the beginnings of some of our canary breeds began to emerge as local groups of fanciers started to develop special characteristics in their birds. It was discovered, for instance, that by selective breeding the canary could become long and slim, short and stocky, a better songster or more brilliantly coloured. This range of variation was further extended by the appearance of mutations which added such features as a crest on the head, frilled feathering on the body, an unusual posture, or distinctive patterning of the plumage.

The perfecting of these emergent breeds was achieved largely through the efforts of fanciers in the nineteenth century. Certain centres of canary culture became noted for their birds; for example, the Roller Canaries of Germany, the Frilled and Posture breeds of the Low Countries, the regional type breeds of Britain, and so on. Most of these breeds are still in existence today, enjoying varying degrees of popularity, but the twentieth century has also seen the continuation of

CE
9.95

THE
COMPLETE
BOOK OF
CANARIES

THE COMPLETE BOOK OF CANARIES

G. T. DODWELL

CONSULTANT EDITOR: KEN DENHAM
EDITED BY ROSEMARY LOW

KIRKCALDY DISTRICT LIBRARIES

636707

636.6862/DOD

Ce

MEREHURST PRESS
LONDON

Front jacket:
Lancashire Plainhead Canary
(Photographed by Cyril Laubscher)

Back jacket:
Lizard Canaries in the 1880s
(from Cassell's "Book of Canaries and Cage-Birds")

Published 1986 by Merehurst Press
5 Great James Street
London WC1N 3DA

© Copyright 1986 Merehurst Limited

ISBN 0 948075 02 3

All rights reserved. No part of this publication may be reproduced,
stored in a retrieval system, or transmitted in any form or by any
means, electronic, mechanical, photocopying, recording, or otherwise,
without the prior written permission of the copyright owner.

Typeset by Lineage
Printed in Hong Kong by South China Printing Company
Colour separation by Fotographics Ltd, London–Hong Kong
Designed by Roger Daniels

ACKNOWLEDGEMENTS
We would like to thank the following for their help in the preparation of this book:
Gordon Plumb; Harry Williamson; Gerry Wolfendale; Jenny Vaughan; Aquila
Photographics; M. Gilroy; Cyril Laubscher; Tony Tilford; Su Martin; Cage and
Aviary Birds Magazine; Porter's Cage Bird Fanciers' Stores; American Cage Bird
Magazine; Arthur Freud; Judy Snider; Donald Perez; William Reichert; Thomas
Baugh; Steve Spencer; Stephen Day; Fife Fancy Canary Club; Gloster Fancy
Convention; National Roller Canary Society; Old Varieties Canary Association;
Red Canary Association; Red Factor Canary Club of Australia; Southern Border
Fancy Canary Club; Southern Norwich Plainhead Canary Club; Southern
Yorkshire Canary Club; Graham Suttle; Albert Newsham; Buster Geary; Tish Harnett;
Cyril Newick; Gary McCarthy; Donato Sepe.

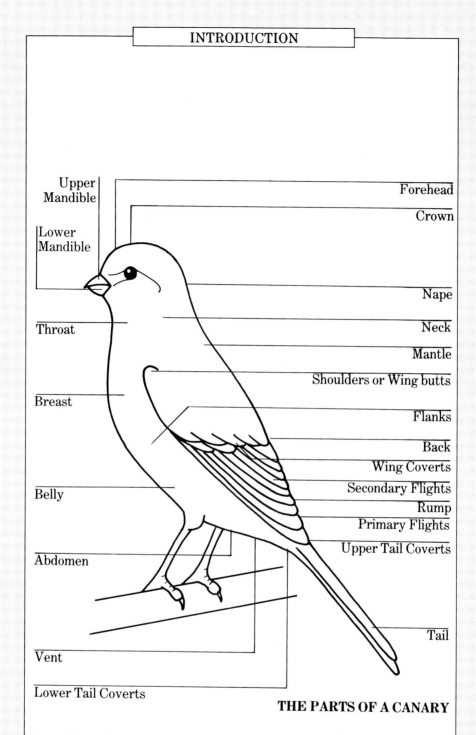

Upper Mandible

Forehead

Crown

Lower Mandible

Nape

Throat

Neck

Mantle

Shoulders or Wing butts

Breast

Flanks

Back

Wing Coverts

Secondary Flights

Belly

Rump

Primary Flights

Upper Tail Coverts

Abdomen

Tail

Vent

Lower Tail Coverts

THE PARTS OF A CANARY

ingenuity and imagination on the part of fanciers which has resulted in several new breeds.

Any person entering into the canary fancy today therefore has a wide range of choice for his activities. They range from the worthwhile preservation of some of the older and rarer breeds to the exciting sphere of new colour mutations which are constantly occurring.

Exhibiting has always been considered an important aspect of any fancy, be it in the realm of horticulture or small livestock, and thus much of what is written in the following pages has this in view as the ultimate objective for most fanciers. However, exhibiting is by no means essential to the enjoyment of canaries, and many people take pleasure merely in their breeding or even in the possession of a single pet songster. For these enthusiasts, too, there is ample information to assist them to care for their charges to the best advantage.

A

ACCESSORIES

Apart from the fundamental housing requirements of cages and a room in which to keep the birds, many other items of equipment are needed in order to carry out the hobby of canary keeping with maximum efficiency. Such items are usually referred to collectively as *accessories* or *appliances*. They may range from those that are in regular use throughout the year, such as seed hoppers, drinkers, baths and grit containers, to those of seasonal application. Examples are nesting pans, nest linings, dummy eggs and feeding trays during the breeding season and training cages, show cages and carrying cases during the show season. Mention will be made of each of these articles under the appropriate heading.

AGATE

(see colour feature pages 22-23)

The breeding of Coloured Canaries is a somewhat specialized activity in which a basic knowledge of genetics is an advantage, if it is intended to include the many different mutations that have occurred. The Agate was the earliest recorded mutation in the modern history of the canary, having occurred in Holland in the year 1900. Until fairly recently it was known in Britain as Dilute Green, which states exactly what it is, a green canary in which the melanin pigments are in a diluted or paler form. The original European term Agate has now been universally adopted and is used in conjunction with the bird's basic ground colour to give Gold Agate (yellow ground), Silver Agate (white ground), Red Agate (red ground), Rose Agate (rose ground), and so on. They are all very attractively coloured.

The Agate is one of many mutations in the canary that are sex-linked, which means its mode of inheritance is dependent upon the sex of the individual (see under *SEX-LINKAGE* for further explanation). Matings and expectations involving Agate birds are as follows:

1 Agate cock x Agate hen: gives all Agate young;
2 Agate cock x normal hen: gives Agate hens and cocks that are visually normal but are carriers of the Agate gene;
3 Normal cock x Agate hen: gives all normal young but the cocks are Agate carriers;
4 Normal cock carrying Agate x Agate hen: gives Agate cocks, normal cocks carrying Agate, Agate hens and normal hens;
5 Normal cock carrying Agate x normal hen: gives normal cocks, normal cocks carrying Agate, normal hens and Agate hens.

AGE

After their first year it is almost impossible to tell a canary's age with any accuracy, although very old birds can usually be recognized by their rough plumage, particularly in the flight and tail feathers. More especially the legs and feet become distinctly more scaly with the advance of age.

Upon leaving their nest at the age of three weeks, young canaries are fully fledged and provided with a set of feathers that will last them until the first moult begins. At this stage of their lives they are known as *nest feather* birds.

During the first moult, which commences when they are about 10 to 12 weeks old, all these nest feathers are replaced, with the exception of the flight feathers of the wings and the tail feathers. The birds are then referred to as *unflighted* (i.e., their flight feathers have not been moulted).

During the following year's moult all feathers are renewed, including the wings and tail, and the canary then becomes a *flighted* bird (the term *overyear* is also used).

This process of feather replacement is repeated annually

AGE CHARACTERISTICS IN THE CANARY

TERM USED	AGE	CHARACTERISTICS
Nest feather	Up to about 10 or 12 weeks	Rather soft, fluffy feathers. Legs and feet pale pink (in clear or lightly marked birds) and somewhat translucent and delicate looking.
Unflighted	3 to 15 months	Flight and tail feathers almost white, with only a slight margin of colour. Legs and feet more robust and not scaly. Nails short.
Flighted, or overyear	15 months onwards	Flight and tail feathers showing more pigment. Legs and feet more scaly as bird gets older. Nails thicker and longer (unless trimmed).

These characteristics are given as a general guide only. Often they are not very well marked and may be difficult to differentiate even by an experienced fancier.

Age given is approximate only as individuals may vary.

but there are no further special terms employed and, however old a bird may become, it is still a flighted specimen. (See also *LONGEVITY*.)

(see colour feature page 90)

AMERICAN SINGER
Some years ago, in the USA, fanciers set out to produce a new breed of canary that would be uniquely their own. The basis for this was to be a blending of the song of the Roller combined with the type and quality of the Border Fancy. Thus the American Singers Club came to be founded.

In the official statement of intent the new breed was descibed as 'a song-type canary bred in the United States by a systematic plan of the blending of Roller to Border Fancy over a period of years to produce a canary that has:
1 An outstanding, free, harmonious song, pleasing to the ear, neither too loud nor too harsh, with plenty of variety;
2 A beautiful shape or type not over 5¾ inches long, with tight feather that will please the average home lover of canaries.'
A planned breeding programme was worked out for the Club's members in which it was calculated that a strain of birds could be produced within five years containing 69% of Roller blood and 31% of Border Fancy. In general appearance this bird takes very much after the Border and, naturally, inherits some of its more strident song. It is officially stated that that the song should be neither Border nor Roller, too much of a tendency in either direction being considered a fault.

Like the Roller, the American Singer should perform freely when being judged and is allowed up to 10 minutes to do so when set before his adjudicator. The standard laid down by the American Singers Club is as follows:

Freedom of Song	10 points
Rendition of Song	60 points
Conformation of Body	20 points
Condition	10 points

APPLE
Canaries enjoy having a slice of sweet apple to peck at if it is pushed between the wires of their cage. It makes an change from the greenstuff and, although its feeding value is not high, it is a useful source of Vitamin C.

Example of an outdoor aviary suitable for housing canaries or a mixed collection of birds

APPLIANCES — See *ACCESSORIES*

AVIARIES

The place for keeping a number of birds is usually thought of as being an aviary, which by definition, is a structure which allows the inmates complete freedom of flight within the limits of the space provided. However, for the breeder of exhibition type canaries, this is not a suitable place at all. The close control and carefully planned matings, which are essential for success on the show bench, can only be exercised if cages are used, for in the environment of an aviary the birds will pick their own partners.

This is not to say that a garden aviary, containing a suitable selection of canaries, cannot be made into an attractive feature and become an endless source of pleasure. Many types are available, either direct from the manufacturers or at garden centres, or aviaries can be constructed at home to suit the space available.

Some serious fanciers, however, do make use of what are termed *FLIGHTS* (which see), either indoor or outdoor, as a part of their birdrooms. In these they may overwinter some of their breeding stock, or keep surplus non-breeding birds during the summer. Such flights, which are in effect miniature aviaries, do allow for greater flexibility in the number of birds being kept. Care should be taken not to overstock one's establishment as this inevitably leads to carrying a number of unwanted, and often inferior, birds.
(See also: *BIRDROOMS.*)

AWARDS

The system of making awards at shows is different in English speaking countries from that practised on the continent of Europe. In Britain and most countries outside Europe the judge works on the basis of a visual comparison of the birds in each class. He places them in order of merit according to how closely each exhibit conforms to the accepted standard of its breed. If numbers are sufficient seven placings are made — First, Second, Third, Fourth, Very Highly Commended (V.H.C.), Highly Commended (H.C.), and Commended (C.). It is becoming a more common practice, however, that these last three courtesy awards are known simply as Fifth, Sixth and Seventh.

At small shows, entries are sometimes very limited, occasionally with only one bird in a class — which still gets its First or Red Ticket. This is clearly nothing of a criterion, as the bird may be an inferior exhibit!

Having dealt with all of his classes, the judge then takes the individual winners and moves on to make the special awards, known to fanciers simply as *Specials*. These usually include the categories of Best Unflighted, Best Flighted, Best Novice, Best Champion, Best of Breed, Best Opposite Sex and so on. Another award that is generally made at most shows is that of Best Canary in Show where each of the breed champions are judged together.

(Photographed by Cage and Aviary)

Border Fancy Canary in its show cage decorated with awards

On the continent of Europe the system of points judging prevails. The birds are not judged against each other but against the scale of points allocated to each particular breed by the controlling authority which is usually the *Confederation Ornithologique Mondiale*.

Each bird's score sheet is marked up by the judge as he assesses its merits and totals the points at the bottom. It is quite possible under this system, in the large classes that often exist, for there to be several first prize birds within the class, each scoring exactly the same number of points.

B

BATHS

Most canaries enjoy bathing at almost any time and, if a bath is not provided for them, they will generally dip their heads into their water vessels. This is less satisfactory than a proper bath which is always followed by vigorous preening, resulting in a good tone to the plumage. Small numbers of birds can easily be provided with a daily bath when the weather is suitable. It is more difficult with a large stock on account of the number of bathing vessels needed and the time consumed in clearing up afterwards. The birds make quite a mess of their cages and the birdroom floor by splashing water all over the place. For this reason many fanciers restrict the baths to once a week — usually just before the routine cleaning of cages and birdroom takes place.

Special bath cages available from most fanciers' suppliers can be hung on the door of the birds' stock cages. These are possibly the best proposition, although any dish-like receptacle can be placed inside the cage to equally good purpose. In either case the depth of water should never be more than 2.5cm (1in) as it is possible for birds to drown. In the past, fanciers often collected clean rainwater for their birds' baths, alleging that it provided an additional sheen to the plumage but, in these days of atmospheric pollution tap water is best.

It is useful to have a fair number of baths available, but not essential. Since they take up a lot of storage space, many fanciers make do with a limited number, hanging them on to a cage just before cleaning begins. Then, while this first cage is being cleaned the baths, replenished

(Photographed by Cage and Aviary)

Modern plastic bath in position on the cage front

(see colour feature page 126)

with clean water, can be hung on to the next cage, and so on, in succession. If a bird does not bath while it has the opportunity there is no need to depart from routine; some birds are less frequent bathers than others.

BELGIAN CANARY

This is one of the oldest and most famous breeds of canary which reached the peak of its development and popularity during Victorian times. Since the turn of the century it has suffered a steady decline. This can be attributed to a variety of reasons, not least of which are the two world wars which have been fought across its Belgian homeland. Its continued use by fanciers for the purpose of improving other breeds was another contributory factor to its decreasing numbers. Nowadays it is a relatively scarce breed, even in its land of origin.

The early history of the Belgian has been unrecorded but evidently it descended from a race of canaries that had existed in the Low Countries during the latter part of the eighteenth century. Its development proceeded with some purpose, aided apparently by the guilds that had existed since medieval times in the towns and cities of Belgium. As a result of the standards laid down, a highly fancy variety of canary had been developed by the middle of the nineteenth century. It was admired by fanciers everywhere

and, in England, was accorded the title of 'King of the Fancy'.

The Belgian of the present day is a degenerate form when compared with its predecessors. The fact that it exists at all is entirely due to the efforts of dedicated fanciers who have had to reconstruct the breed from less than satisfactory material. As time goes by and the process of selection continues, it is to be hoped that this famous old breed of canary may regain something of its former status.

The name by which the Belgian was known in its earlier days was *potuurvogel* which indicates that it was a *posture bird* or *bird of position*. This means that it should be able to take up a special attitude when in the show cage in order to display its various fancy points to best advantage. These points, taken together, form its basic type and are then displayed to perfection as the bird adopts its show position.

To the untutored eye this is quite remarkable. The bird grips the perch firmly and pulls itself up to its maximum height with the line of the back being perfectly upright — this being an essential point in a show Belgian. The head and neck at the same time are actually being lowered with the neck stretched out to its full length and the bird looking downwards to the bottom of the cage. It will be appreciated that, in this attitude, the shoulders will be at the highest point, and this accounts for the name by which this breed is known in Europe, namely *Bossu Belge*, or *Belgische Bult*, meaning 'Belgian Humpback'.

Official Standard

The standard that is applied for the judging of Belgian canaries is that approved by the *Confederation Ornithologique Mondiale*. It reads as follows:

1 Position	*Points*
POSITION — Comfortable and confident	10
NECK — Fine and well elongated	10
LEGS — Upright and stiff	4
SHOULDERS — High	10
HEAD — Lowered	6

2 Form

HEAD — Small, oval narrow and
sleek   3
NECK — Long, refined and
extended   10
SHOULDERS — High, well set and
well filled   10
BACK — Long, broad, well filled
and upright   5
BODY — Long and tapering   5
BREAST — Prominent and well
filled   5
WINGS — Long, tightly folded and
touching without crossing   5
TAIL — Long, upright, closely
folded stiff and closed at the tip   3
LEGS — Long, slim and upright   4
PLUMAGE — Smooth, without frills
                                                6
SIZE — 17 to 18cm from the tip of
the beak to the end of the tail   4
                                    Total 100

BERNESE CANARY

This breed, one of several minority
varieties recognized by the
*Confederation Ornithologique
Mondiale*, is not particularly
common even in Europe and is
virtually unknown elsewhere. In
form it is not unlike the earliest
types of Yorkshire Canary —
judging by illustrations of the
latter in Victorian treatises on
canaries.

Official Standard

The standard applied by the
C.O.M. is as follows:
HEAD — Narrow, long and
flattened, crown projecting to the

rear to form an angle with the neck
NECK — Sturdy of medium length
BREAST — Full and well developed
THIGHS — Moderately visible
LEGS — Slightly bent
WING BUTTS — Clearly visible
BACK — Long and slightly rounded
WINGS — Long and well set
TAIL — Long and straight
BODY — Tapering, cone shaped
PLUMAGE — Smooth and close
POSITION — Almost upright
COLOUR — Uniform, yellow or
variegated
SIZE — 16 to 17.5cm

	Points
POSITION	20
HEAD AND NECK	20
BREAST/SHOULDERS/BACK	20
WINGS AND TAIL	10
LEGS AND FEET	10
PLUMAGE AND COLOUR	10
GENERAL CONDITION	10
	Total 100

BIRDROOMS

Although canaries can be kept
fairly successfully in all sorts of
places, such as out-houses, disused
garages, home extension units and
converted greenhouses, the
provision of a properly constructed
birdroom should be the aim of
every aspiring fancier. Here the
birds' relatively simple basic needs
can be catered for at the outset
rather than being adapted from an
existing building. It should be said,
however, that if there is no choice
in the matter, or if cost is a limiting
factor, the enthusiast need not be
deterred from taking up canaries.
Many a seemingly unlikely place
can be made into quite comfortable
quarters with a little ingenuity,
provided that a few simple points
are observed.

Whether providing a completely
new structure for the birds or
adapting alternative
accommodation, the guiding
principles should be the same. A
birdroom should be:
1 Free from damp;
2 Free from draughts;
3 Properly ventilated;
4 Well insulated;
5 Adequately lit;
6 Vermin-proof.

If there is any choice in the matter, it should be situated to receive the benefit of morning sunshine and yet avoid the full heat of a hot summer's day.

The majority of birdrooms are practical structures, usually basically of a garden shed design, with additional window space for extra lighting. If something more attractive is required, it can be in the form of a summerhouse or garden chalet, either of which can look ornamental as well as being pr_ .ical. The birdroom should be of sufficient size to accommodate the number of birds that it is intended to keep, without overcrowding. The newcomer to the fancy often finds that he has

(Photographed by Cage and Aviary)

A well ordered bird room planned for efficient management

soon outgrown the original space he provided.

As a general guide, a shed of 2.4m x 1.8m (8ft x 6ft) would be adequate for six breeding pairs and their maximum expected progeny in one year — say a total of 45 to 50 birds. Similarly a shed of 3.6m x 3m (12ft x 10ft) would be needed for 60 to 65 birds, or the equivalent of eight breeding pairs.

It is rare, of course, for all pairs to fulfil their maximum potential but the fancier should avoid having too many pairs as, in a good season, it may lead to serious, over-crowding of the stock. The numbers quoted above could be accommodated only by utilizing three sides of the birdroom and having all windows and the door at the front.

Birdrooms can be constructed of any suitable material for outdoor use. A brick building would be ideal, but expensive, and so a timber-framed structure with wooden boarding is used by the majority of fanciers. Such a building needs an inside lining and efficient insulation, especially in the roof, where heat loss is noticeable in the winter and where heat penetrates in the summer. The room should preferably be raised well clear of the ground upon brick or concrete pillars in order to avoid any rising damp.

It is important to have free ventilation so that fresh air can circulate without producing draughts. To this end, air intakes can be constructed just above floor level and underneath the lowest line of cages. The outlets can be situated high up above the topmost cages. If these ventilators are fitted with sliding covers they can be closed in cold or windy weather. An added refinement could be provided in the form of an extractor fan to aid circulation, especially in sultry weather.

Adequate lighting to all parts of the birdroom is important for the well-being of canaries and so plenty of window space is recommended. The provision of artificial lighting, however, is a doubtful undertaking, although many fanciers need to install it in order to attend to their stock during the winter. If this has to be done, they should use it as little as possible. If it is left on too much, it may bring the birds into premature breeding condition. Some fanciers do this intentionally and carry out an early breeding programme with the aid of both artificial lighting and heating.

The question of heat in the birdroom will be largely a matter of geography; in countries with a severe winter it is essential. It is sensible to keep the birdroom temperature above freezing point in winter in all climates, in order to prevent the drinking water from becoming frozen. To this end an electric tubular heater with thermostatic control is the most

OVERCOMING PROBLEMS IN THE BIRDROOM

PROBLEM	CURE
Damp	Brick structure – proper damp-proof course. Wooden shed – raised well clear of ground. Adequate overhang at eaves and/or efficient guttering and downpipe.
Draught	Well fitting doors and windows. Use of draught-proof strips.
Ventilation	Ventilators near floor and ceiling. Not to be in such a position as to place cages in a draught.
Insulation	Walls and roof lined. Space between filled with insulating material.
Light	Adequately sized windows. Avoid shading by large trees or tall buildings.
Vermin	Mouse guards. Small mesh wire netting around base of structure. Similar netting frames for windows and doors (mesh larger than 10mm (⅜in) square admits mice).

satisfactory form of heating. It relieves the fancier of the worry that his birds may be without water. In hot climates, air conditioning and humidity controls are often necessary. In such places, there are often mosquitoes and similar insects which may harm canaries. In this case, windows and doors will need to be covered with suitable screens, just as human dwellings have to be protected in the same circumstances.

BLUE CANARIES

If Blue Canaries are mentioned to the non-fancier, they are incredulous; nevertheless blue canaries do exist — not the clear bright blue of the Budgerigar but more of a slate-blue shade. The Blue Canary has the same basic melanin pigments as the green but, since in this case they are superimposed upon a white ground colour instead of yellow, the slate-blue coloration is induced. Self blues, as well as blue-marked and blue-variegated whites, are to be found in most of the existing breeds of canary although, on the whole, they are not so popular as the normals. If any fancier wishes to take up the breeding of blues there is no great difficulty in running them along with a normal stock of canaries — the genetic relationship is relatively simple. The one great exception to this is in the case of the Lizard Canary. Blue Lizards have, from time to time been produced, but as they obviously represent the intrusion of outside blood into a pure and ancient breed, they are frowned upon.

BORDER FANCY

Foremost in popularity among the type breeds of canary is the Border Fancy. It owes its existence to fanciers on either side of the Anglo-Scottish border, the particular border referred to in the title. The epithet *fancy*, which also appears in the title of several other British breeds, signifies a specially cultivated show type of bird as opposed to the ordinary undeveloped specimen. In this connection the *Concise Oxford Dictionary* defines 'fancy' as 'bred for particular points of beauty based upon complicated or arbitrary qualifications'.

The origins of the Border lie in the ordinary domestic canaries that were kept by fanciers in the border counties of England and Scotland. They were exhibited at shows whenever separate classes were provided for 'Common Canaries' as distinct from the currently established breeds. They gradually developed and perfected

(see colour feature pages 18-19)

their birds into a refined and acceptable type. A specialist society was formed at Hawick in 1890 when the title Border Fancy was adopted.

The newly-formed society had a membership of just 43, but today the Border has risen to such heights of popularity that it is kept by thousands of fanciers in all parts of the world.

The early type of Border soon became known in the fancy as the 'Wee Gem'. Indeed, it was both tiny and jewel-like in character, being bright, lively and confident in manner, not unlike today's Fife Fancy. The ideals of fanciers, however, do not remain static and, over the years, the Border has undergone some changes and has developed into a larger and more robust breed, although still retaining most of the original characteristics.

The Border probably represents the general public's idea of what a canary should look like. It is a plain, neat, 'no-nonsense' bird without any fancy characteristics such as a crest, frilled feathering or unusual posture. It is often recommended as being an ideal breed for the beginner and this, to some extent, is true. Unlike some breeds, Borders are always freely available at reasonable prices from pet shops, bird dealers and breeders. When the beginner joins his local cage bird society, he will find a fair sprinkling of Border men among its membership who are sure to be ready with help and advice. It must be added, however, that top-quality exhibition birds are just as difficult to achieve in this as in any other breed.

Official Standard

The general appearance is that of a clean-cut, lightly-made, compact, proportionable, close-feathered canary, showing no tendency to heaviness, roughness or dullness, but giving the impression of fine quality and symmetry throughout.

Points

HEAD — Small, round and neat looking, beak fine, eyes central to roundness of head and body   10

BODY — Back well filled and nicely rounded, running in almost a straight line from the gentle rise over the shoulders to the point of the tail. Chest also nicely rounded, but neither heavy nor prominent, the line gradually tapering to the vent   15

WINGS — Compact and carried close to the body, just meeting at the tips, at a little lower than the root of the tail   10

LEGS — Of medium length, showing little thigh, fine, and in harmony with the other points, yet corresponding   5

PLUMAGE — Close, firm, fine in quality, presenting a smooth, glossy, silken appearance, free from frill or roughness   10

TAIL — Close packed and narrow, being nicely rounded and filled in at the root   5

POSITION — Semi-erect, standing at an angle of 60 degrees

CARRIAGE — Gay, jaunty, with full poise of the head   15

COLOUR — Rich, soft and pure, as level in tint as possible throughout but extreme depth and hardness, such as colour feeding gives are debarred   15

HEALTH —Condition and cleanliness shall have due weight   10

SIZE — But not to exceed 5½ inches length   5

Total 100

BREEDING

The breeding season is the cornerstone of the canary fancier's hobby. Success or failure at this stage will determine what he will have available for the autumn shows. It will also decide whether he will be in a position to advance his breeding programme in the following year with home-bred birds, or have to purchase replacement stock.

Breeding is such an important aspect of the hobby, and so capable of diversification in its approach, that only a few of the basic points are dealt with under this entry. The many other facets of breeding will appear under specific headings but, even here, no writer could possibly claim to cover every eventuality.

Fanciers are constantly learning and adjusting their methods as they go along; taking up new approaches, new feeding, new matings, and so on. Even fanciers of 50 years' experience will admit that they do not know all of the answers — and never will of course! Good seasons, bad seasons, indifferent seasons come and go, often with no apparent explanation for the variations in results. The outcome of any given breeding season is quite unpredictable, but

Pair of canaries at their nest

herein lies the fascination of canary breeding. Every season starts from scratch and there is always the exciting possibility of breeding something really good.

In his very first season the newcomer will probably be starting with correctly matched pairs of birds which have been supplied to him by an established fancier. It will have been pointed out to him that, in canary breeding, it is the usual practice to have a pair made up of one Yellow and one Buff bird (either a Yellow cock matched with a Buff hen, or vice versa).

In most breeds of the type canaries, markings are of little importance and the birds may be Clear, Ticked, Marked, Variegated, Green or Cinnamon — it is largely a matter of personal preference, although most fanciers like to keep a balance so that they have reasonable numbers in each category from which to select their show teams. (Definitions of these technical terms are dealt with under their specific headings).

Although most fanciers work

with pairs of birds, it is quite a common practice to have breeding trios consisting of one cock bird mated to two hens. This is not a particularly difficult system to handle (see *DOUBLE PAIRING*) but any newcomer would be better advised to start with the simple method of single pairing which will present him with fewer problems.

Most beginners are naturally impatient to get started when spring comes around and there is a great temptation to pair up too soon. The correct time to start breeding, as all old hands will confirm, is when the birds are ready. This is a sufficiently vague statement to be of little help to the inexperienced. But, if the birds have been properly prepared, with a gradual build-up from late winter onwards, it will generally be found that they are in fit condition early in spring assuming that no artificial aids in the way of heating or lighting have been given.

By this time the cocks will be singing lustily for most of the day, usually with the body swaying from side to side as they sing and with a restless marking time with the feet or moving to and fro along the perch. When not engaged in singing they will be attempting to gain a view of any hens in nearby cages by putting their heads close to the wires of their cages or through the drinker holes.

The hens will be showing a general air of restlessness by flying ceaselessly from end to end of their cages or flapping their wings even when standing still. They will constantly be calling to the cocks and may be seen to be carrying nesting material about in their beaks. Some hens will start to form nests by creating little depressions in the sawdust in the corner of the cage. The ultimate expression of their readiness to breed, however, is when they crouch low upon the perch with tail raised inviting the act of coition, whenever they hear the vigorous singing of a cock bird in a neighbouring cage. When these signs are noticed no time should be lost in introducing the pair to each other.

Border Fancy

White Border
Fancy Canary

Player's Cigarettes

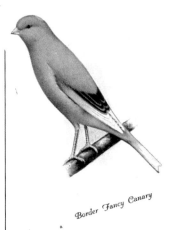

Border Fancy Canary

Modern example of
a Border Fancy
Canary

Membership badge
of the Southern
Border Fancy Club
of Great Britain

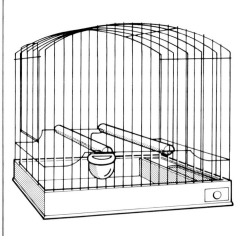

Standard show
cage approved by
the Border
Convention of
specialist societies

(Photograph by Cyril Laubscher)

Early Border
Fancies from "Our
Canaries" (1911)

The breeding season should then proceed throughout the spring and should finish by mid-summer. During this period two or three broods should have been raised, according to circumstances. All young birds should have been weaned and be quite independent of their parents by the end of summer.

BUFF

In the canary there are two basic types of feather quality to be found which are known to fanciers as Yellow and Buff. In both types the lipochrome colouring is, in fact, yellow but in the Buff birds the yellow pigment is less intense than in the Yellow. It does not extend

quite to the extreme margin of the feathers, where the absence of colouring results in a narrow edging of white. This gives to the bird a lightly frosted, or mealy appearance which is usually more noticeable in hens than in cocks.

In dark pigmented birds, such as Greens, the Buff type of bird is recognizable by having a greyish edging to the feather. Apart from the differences in pigmentation between the Yellow and Buff feathers there are slight structural differences too, those of the Buffs being somewhat larger, broader and softer in texture. This tends to make the Buff appear generally a little bolder and fuller in figure, although in birds of exceptional quality the difference may be slight. In Coloured Canaries the Buffs are known as *Non-intensive*, although sometimes the older term of *Frosted* is still used. In Lizard Canaries the Buff birds are termed *Silver* which must not be confused with the use of the word *Silver* in Coloured Canary circles which refers to birds with a white ground colour.

CAGES

Apart from the *BIRDROOM* accommodation (which see) it is in cages that canaries will spend most of their lives. These therefore become the most important item of equipment for the fancier to provide. Whether he purchases them ready-made or makes them himself, they may prove to be an expensive part of his initial outlay. However, with care, the cages may last a lifetime in the hobby.

Specialized types of cage (show cages, for example) are needed at certain seasons of the year but, for permanent use in the birdroom, a simple utility pattern has been used by fanciers over the years. Although anyone may follow his own inclinations in the matter, it is probably better to follow tradition and keep to a design that has been proved by experience to be most satisfactory.

These widely-used cages are known as *box cages* in which all but the wire front is made of wood. According to the length in which they are made, they can be divided off into any number of compartments which can be separated by means of permanent, or preferably movable, partitions. Because they are used as breeding units during the appropriate season, these cages are known to fanciers as *breeders* — single breeders, double breeders, treble breeders, and so on, according to the number of compartments in which they are constructed.

The most widespread is the double breeder which is not only a convenient size to handle but may readily be converted for other purposes. It will accommodate one breeding pair and their offspring prior to weaning. Out of season, it will be useful as a stock cage for a couple of adult cocks (usually

Double breeding
cage of the box
type

separated by a slide) or by a small group of hens. Similarly, a small number of youngsters can be housed during their first moult. In addition to these, many fanciers also like to have a few cages of greater length, called *flight cages*, to provide some extra exercise for their stock.

A useful standard size for a double breeder is 90cm (3ft) long, 40cm (16in) in height and 30cm (12in) deep. Slight variations enable the cages to fit neatly and without waste of space into the shape of the birdroom. It is advisable to make the cages to a uniform pattern so that they may be removed and interchanged at any time without upsetting the routine. If any of the larger breeds of canary are kept it is desirable, though not essential, to have slightly larger cages.

Sound construction and careful workmanship will ensure that there are no badly fitting joints where insect pests might hide. Some fanciers carry the utility principle to the limit by leaving their cages finished in plain wood which can then be regularly treated with a wood preservative and/or insect repellant. The majority, however, prefer to see their cages looking more attractive and so paint them with a matt emulsion paint in a light colour — pale blue, pale green or white being the most popular.

As an alternative to separate cages, a built-in cage system can readily be devised and prove perfectly efficient. This would take the form of a series of shelves spaced 40cm (16in) apart, each shelf being 30cm (12in) wide. The spaces between would then be divided into compartments of the required length and wire fronts

attached by means of a supporting strip of wood. These wire fronts for cages are supplied in various sizes from fanciers' stores but they can be made by hand if desired.

In the USA and continental Europe many fanciers use open wire cages of a simple design that can be accommodated on the stacking principle. Dimensions for these are the same as for box cages, although variations are possible to suit individual requirements.

It is important to start the hobby with sufficient cage accommodation to allow for the growing crop of youngsters. If a start is made with, say, two breeding pairs of birds it is suggested that six double breeders of the type described would be advisable to accommodate the parents and their expected progeny.

Pet canaries are usually kept in open wire cages but of a more ornamental design than those used by practical breeders. Further details of these are given under *PET CANARY*.

CANARY SEED
To the uninitiated, canary seed is merely a packet of mixed seed for feeding canaries that can be obtained from pet shops or supermarkets. To the fancier, it is one kind of seed only, that of the canary grass *Phalaris canariensis*. It forms the principal item in the bird's staple diet. It is quite an important crop in such Mediterranean countries as Turkey and Morocco and is also widely grown in Australia, Canada and the USA. These various seeds probably vary slightly in quality and feeding value according to source and from season to season. Generally this is

Coloured Canaries

Top: Silver Brown Satinette

Above: Non-Frosted Bronze

Left: Frosted Gold Isabel Pastel

22

Non-Frosted
Blue Opal

Player's Cigarettes

Green Canary

Common Green
Canary from which
most of the colour
mutations have
descended

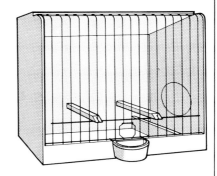

Official show cage
in which all of the
many colour
varieties are now
exhibited

Left: Non-Frosted
Green

Far Left: Non-
Frosted Rose
Agate

of little consequence if obtained from a reputable seedsman who would ensure that all samples were satisfactory.

Some fanciers like to have nothing but canary seed in the seed hoppers at all times, giving additional food items in separate vessels as required. It is, however, a more usual practice to use a basic mixture of three parts of canary seed and one part of rape seed which gives a better balance of proteins, carbohydrates and fats.

CAP
The cap is a specialized feature of the Lizard Canary in which there is an area of light feathers covering the crown of the head of these birds, whose plumage is otherwise dark. In the ideal it should be of an oval or thumbnail shape approximately following the line of the skull. There should be a clearly defined edge extending from the base of the upper mandible to the back of the skull and passing just above the eye from which it is separated by a thin line of dark feathers called the eyelash. (See *LIZARD CANARY*.)

CAPPED or CAP-MARKED
These terms are used in breeds, other than the Lizard, for birds that have a dark patch of feathering on the crown of their heads. The marking may be relatively small or similar in extent to the Lizard's cap. In these other breeds a cap marking is of no special significance and is merely a localized manifestation of variegation.

A cap-marked bird which also shows some variegation on other parts of its body

CARROT
Carrot can be used as an occasional change from greenfoods. It can be grated, or a slice can be placed between the bars of the cage. Some old canary manuals also advocated giving a piece of boiled carrot during the moult as an aid to improving the colour of the bird, and to enhance the sheen on the plumage. It is doubtful whether many of today's fanciers do this, but there is certainly no harm in trying it.

CHAMPION
Unlike some branches of livestock, where it is the animal itself that acquires champion status, here it is the breeder. In the canary fancy there are only two categories of exhibitor that are recognized — the Novice and the Champion, the former graduating to the latter after fulfilling a reasonable number of conditions. The generally accepted ruling defining a champion is an exhibitor who has attained a certain measure of success in the hobby by winning three or more first prizes as a novice in Open competition.

There is usually a saving clause that states that any prizes won in classes where there are less than three exhibitors participating, or where there are less than seven staged exhibits, can be disregarded. So, too, are any wins in selling classes or at any event that is not fully open, such as a member's show of a local club. Thus it is quite possible for a fancier to remain a novice for a number of years if the right conditions are not fulfilled. In fact, many novices may choose to move up to champion status voluntarily after a period of time. Some of the specialist societies place a time-limit for a member remaining a novice.

CINNAMON
This was the first sport as regards colour to appear in the canary, being mentioned in a treatise as long ago as 1709. We now know that it arose as a result of a mutation in the gene producing *melanin* (dark) pigments in the

EXPECTATION FROM GREEN AND CINNAMON MATINGS

	PARENTS	PROGENY
1	Green cock x Green hen	All Green
2	Cinnamon cock x Cinnamon hen	All Cinnamon
3	Green cock x Cinnamon hen	All Green, but cocks will be Cinnamon carriers
4	Cinnamon cock x Green hen	Green cocks (carrying Cinnamon), Cinnamon hens
5	Green cock carrying Cinnamon x Green hen	Green cocks, Green cocks carrying Cinnamon, Green hens, Cinnamon hens
6	Green cock carrying Cinnamon x Cinnamon hen	Green cocks carrying Cinnamon, Cinnamon cocks, Green hens, Cinnamon hens

This table applies whether the birds are self, marked or variegated. Even clear birds follow the same rules, although the only way to distinguish them is by their eye colour – Cinnamons being pink-eyed as against the dark eye colour of the Greens. However, this feature is only readily distinguishable in the nestling stage; it is much more difficult to distinguish in adult birds.

plumage. The ordinary Green Canary possesses black and brown pigments (*eumelanin* and *phaeomelanin*) but in the Cinnamon Canary the black is absent. The remaining brown pigment upon the yellow lipochrome ground colour of the bird gives the familiar shade of yellowish brown that we know as cinnamon.

Cinnamon Canaries are to be found among most breeds and can be incorporated with normal stocks if so desired, although most breeders who go in for Cinnamons tend to specialize in them. This is particularly so in the case of the Norwich Cinnamon, which provides a fascinating field for the breeder as it is now somewhat neglected.

Cinnamons have a mutant gene located on the sex-determining chromosome and thus have what is known as a *sex-linked* form of inheritance. This is explained under the heading of *GENETICS*. A table is appended showing the various matings involving Greens and Cinnamons.

Cocks can be of three kinds — pure breeding Greens, pure Cinnamons, and what are known as *Cinnamon carriers*. Because Cinnamon is recessive to Green, such cocks are visually the same as pure breeding Greens but are in fact carrying the characteristic for Cinnamon which they can pass on to their progeny. Hens must be either Green or Cinnamon — there are no Cinnamon carriers.

CLASSIFICATION

In any form of hobby, whether it be stamp collecting, train spotting or canary breeding, some form of a classification is necessary to advance the knowledge and make the pursuit intelligible to its devotees. With canaries this classification is based upon age, sex, colour and markings so that there is a whole range of recognized categories which cover every type of bird. So far in this book *AGE* and *BUFF* have been dealt with so that the reader will already know, for example, what is meant by an *unflighted buff*. In the accompanying table the full classification is laid out in which all the other technical terms appear.

Gloster Fancy

Cinnamon Consort
Hen

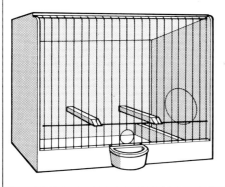

Show cage for the
Gloster Fancy
Canary

Badge of the South
Western Gloster
Club of Great
Britain

Dark Crested Wing
Marked White
Corona Cock

Far left: Yellow
Dark Crested
Corona Cock

Left: Variegated
Buff Consort Cock

These will be described later in this book. The first of these, in fact, follows immediately.

CLEAR

In a Clear canary there should be no dark feathering present so that the bird is quite recognizable as either a Clear Yellow or a Clear Buff. Very occasionally some otherwise Clear birds may possess a certain amount of dark pigment in the *underflue* (the soft, fluffy part of the feather next to the skin) but, so long as it is not seen on the surface as the bird stands normally on its perch, it is generally accepted as a Clear. In addition, any little dark markings that may appear on the legs, feet or beak are usually disregarded in the definition of a Clear.

Clear Buff Border Fancy Canary

CLASSIFICATION

AGE	SEX	COLOUR	MARKINGS
Flighted	Cocks	Yellow	*Clear Ticked Marked Variegated Foul Self
		Buff	*Clear Ticked Marked Variegated Foul Self
	Hens	Yellow	*Clear Ticked Marked Variegated Foul Self
		Buff	*Clear Ticked Marked Variegated Foul Self
Unflighted	Classification the same as for flighted		

*It is rare for the full classification to be used, even at the largest shows, where Clear and Ticked are usually bracketed together; also Marked and Variegated and likewise Foul and Self.

Note: This classification is almost universal but does not apply to Lizard Canaries, nor to Lancashire Canaries where only Clear birds are recognized.

CLUTCH

The clutch size of different species can vary enormously from a single egg to twenty or more. The normal clutch for a canary is four or five. Four is the more usual among the larger breeds and five among the smaller ones.

COLOURS

(See colour feature page 22)

Some mention has already been made of canary colours under the headings of *AGATE*, *BLUE*, *BUFF* and *CINNAMON* and others follow. Basically the colour of the bird is made up of two elements:

1 The ground colour of the feather which may be yellow, white, orange, etc;
2 The dark melanins of black and brown.

These are superimposed in varying degrees upon this ground colour to give Green, Blue, Bronze, Cinnamon, Fawn, Brown, and so on. In most breeds of the ordinary type canaries we usually deal with the normal yellow ground bird, either with Green or Cinnamon markings.

In the Coloured Canary section of the fancy, however, a whole range of mutations have occurred, mostly involving the melanin pigments. There is a bewildering array of differently coloured birds to become familiar with. Many of these are in quite beautiful and delicate shades, previously unheard of in the canary, others perhaps more ordinary or even drab, but all are most interesting. As the field of colour breeding is rather specialized, no attempt will be made to go into detail with the multitude of types (except in the case of the more familiar ones) and so the reader who is attracted to this section of the fancy is advised to consult a standard book on the subject, such as G. B. R. Walker's *Coloured Canaries*.

COLOUR FEEDING

In many breeds of canary, richness of colour is of some importance (very much so in certain varieties) and, all other things being equal, it will turn the scales in the bird's favour on the show bench. It is in the interests of every fancier to do all that he can to enable his birds to achieve a purity and depth of tone that will bring him success. Only at moulting time are the newly developing feathers able to take up the colour-producing substances from the bloodstream. These are supplied by the various items consumed.

It should be emphasized that good colour must first be selected for in breeding. No matter what methods are employed, a bird with a naturally poor colour can never be improved upon beyond a certain point.

The various breeds of canary can here be divided into two groups: those that are shown in the *natural colour*, and those that have to be *colour fed* for exhibition purposes.

In the former category come the Belgian, Border Fancy, Crested Canary, Fife Fancy, Frilled Canaries, Gloster Canary, Lancashire, Scotch Fancy and Roller.

The colour-fed breeds are the Lizard, Norwich, Red Canary and Yorkshire. Special items of food are given to them during the moult which are designed to turn the basic yellow ground colour into a rich orange. Red canaries already have the advantage of being orange, but expert colour feeding can produce a colour very near to red.

The practice of colour feeding has a very long history, dating as far back as the 1870s, when Cayenne pepper was the substance first employed for the purpose. Later, sweet red peppers became the standard colour food ingredient and are still used to this day. A great advance has occurred in comparatively recent times with the discovery of *canthaxanthin*, which is readily available to fanciers. The majority now use it, either on its own or in combination with one of the more traditional colour foods.

Whatever methods are employed, they usually resolve themselves into two basic categories: colour food that is

Lancashire

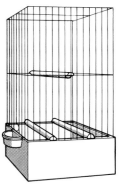

Player's Cigarettes

Lancashire Canary

Lancashire Canaries from a standard text book of the nineteenth century, Cassell's "Book of Canaries and Cage-Birds" illustrated by the famous J. W. Ludlow

Show cage for Lancashire Canaries

Two present day Lancashire Canaries, Coppy left and Plainhead right

(Photograph by Cyril Laubscher)

(Photograph by Cyril Laubscher)

30

Badge of the Old
Varieties Canary
Association which
caters for all of the
old and rare breeds

Lancashire Coppy
Canary in the early
1900s showing the
ideal horseshoe
shaped crest

administered by mixing it dry with a soft food base, and soluble colour food given in the birds' drinking water. Some fanciers use both methods in an effort to get as much colour into their birds as possible, although it is doubtful if this is entirely necessary. It can lead to the colour becoming a burnt orange instead of the bright fiery tone desired.

It is usual to start colour feeding well before the moult actually commences — say, when the youngsters are about eight weeks old. This ensures that the colouring agent can be circulating in the bird's system before any feathers drop. In the case of the soluble colour foods, the manufacturers' directions should be followed. This usually involves starting off with a fairly weak solution which gradually increases to full strength as the moult gets under way.

Dry mixtures which are incorporated in the soft food also start as a weak mix of about one part of colour food to 10 parts of soft food, gradually increasing the strength week by week until it is in the proportion of about one part in four by the time the birds are starting to drop their first feathers. Most forms of soft food should be slightly moistened to a crumbly moist consistency. (See *SOFT FOOD*.)

Colour feeding should continue at full strength throughout the moult, gradually decreasing the amount given as the final feathers are being shed around the head and face. It should not cease altogether, however, until the bird has fully hardened off a few weeks later. Most birds that are robust in constitution will get through the moult and attain tight, hard condition without causing their owners any anxiety.

(see colour feature page 91)

COLUMBUS FANCY
This breed has been developed by fanciers in the USA. It was named after the city of Columbus, in Ohio, where many of its early admirers lived. It has now been taken up by fanciers throughout the USA and is still gaining in popularity.

It is essentially a manufactured breed, in which several English varieties have been blended together, notably the Lancashire Coppy, Gloster Fancy, Norwich and Border Fancy. The two former were obviously the source of the crested gene, for the Columbus Fancy is one of several crested breeds of canary, and as such exists in both crested and plainheaded forms. (See *CREST*.)

As with all other crested breeds, matings are always planned on the basis of crest x plainhead (or plainhead x crest) which produces 50% of each type among the progeny. (The principles involved in this procedure are explained under the heading *GENETICS*.)

The Columbus Fancy is a medium to large-sized canary with a somewhat more upright stance than the Crested Canary which stands at a very low angle across the perch. All of the usual standard canary colours are permitted, but the dark crested birds with clear bodies are especially admired and often seen on the show benches. Two standards are given by the specialist society, one for the crested bird and one for the plainhead:

Official Standard
Crested Columbus Fancy

	Points
CREST (size, shape, droop, size of a half-dollar, round rosette)	45
BODY	10
FEATHER	10
POSITION	10
CONDITION	10
BEAK	5
NECK (fullness)	5
LEGS (short, thighs well clothed)	5
	Total 100

Smooth-head
Columbus Fancy

	Points
HEAD (large, well rounded)	25
BODY (stout, chubby, 5½-6in long)	20
EYEBROWS	10
BEAK (short, neat)	10
FEATHER (leafy texture)	10
SIZE, SHAPE, POSITION	15
HEALTH, CLEANLINESS	10
	Total 100

However, two American authorities, Perez and Reichert, give a different standard in which some emphasis is given to the colour of the bird. They also state that the originator of the breed was Mrs W. A. Finney from Columbus and that the basic material used was the Crested Canary, the Norwich Plainhead and the Hartz, with possibly some miniature Yorkshire blood as well.

CONDITION SEED

This is a mixture of seeds not commonly used in ordinary seed mixtures and may contain dandelion, thistle, lettuce, maw, gold of pleasure and chicory as well as the more usual hemp (if available), teazle, niger, linseed, etc. As its name implies, it is used particularly as a tonic and conditioner for show birds and breeding stock, and to bring birds into top condition at the conclusion of the moult. Many fanciers also like to give a small quantity of condition seed once or twice a week to all of their stock throughout the winter months.

CREST

Although there have been many mutations in the colours of the canary, very few have occurred in the formation and disposition of the feathering. One of these, however, is the crest — a striking adornment which forms the most distinctive feature of the Crested Canary, the Gloster Fancy and the Lancashire and several other breeds such as the Padovan Frill, the German Crest and the Columbus Fancy. The mutation is of very ancient date, having been first mentioned in print in a treatise dated 1793. Basically the crest, which of course adorns the crown of the bird's head, consists of a complete circle of feathers which radiate all round from a central point rather like the spokes of a wheel.

All mutations have a definite genetic relationship with the original unmutated form and are found to conform to a strict mathematical formula during the course of breeding. Thus the crest is of a type known as *heterozygous dominant*. This means that it is dominant to the normal plainheaded bird but is not true breeding, producing only 50% crested progeny and 50% plainheads when mated to a plainhead. When mated crest x crest only 50% crests and 25% plainheads are produced. (The remaining 25% of the progeny are non-viable — see under *GENETICS*.)

For this reason, all crested breeds of the canary consist of the two types of individual: those which actually possess crests on their heads, and those with ordinary plain heads. All bodily characteristics are identical within the breed and it is merely the presence or absence of a crest upon the head that distinguishes the two. In the case of the breed known as the Crested Canary the two forms are known as *Crests* and *Crest-breds*, in the Gloster Fancy as *Coronas* and *Consorts* and in the Lancashire as *Coppies* and *Plainheads*.

In all of the crested breeds of canary it is usual to make up a breeding pair to consist of one crested partner (it makes no difference whether it is the cock or the hen) and one plainhead. As explained above, this gives a result of 50% of each type among the progeny. Sometimes, for special reasons, two crested birds are put together, but because the mutant gene is lethal when present in a double dose, a proportion of their progeny are unable to develop.

CRESTED CANARY

Although it is now in the hands of fewer fanciers than in former times, this is regarded as the foremost of all the crested breeds — hence the almost autocratic assumption of its title the Crested Canary! It started in the middle of

(see colour feature pages 118-19)

the last century as merely a crested form of the Norwich Canary and is still occasionally referred to as the Crested Norwich by some fanciers. It should not be — as it has travelled far along its own road of development since Victorian times.

In those days breeders of the Crested Norwich were inhibited in their efforts to produce larger and better crests by the fine, tight feather quality required on the body. They therefore abandoned this aspect of the bird as a primary aim and concentrated solely upon perfecting the crest. In order to bring about improvements to the small, neat and daisy-like crests of their birds they turned to an outcross with the Lancashire Coppy. This was a huge canary, about 20cm (8in) long, and with a large crest drooping well forward over the beak and eyes.

The result of this introduction of new blood was to be seen in birds that had vastly improved crests but were quite different in bodily conformation from the original Crested Norwich. On the first few occasions that they appeared on the show bench, in fact, they were disqualified by the judges for not being true representatives of their breed.

In due time these new Crested Canaries became acceptable to the fancy and reached limits of development that would have been undreamed of in earlier years. They attracted such attention that very high prices were asked and paid for outstanding birds. This caused their admirers to dub them King of the Canary Fancy — a title formerly accorded to the Belgian.

During the past half-century, for a variety of reasons, the Crested Canary has suffered a gradual decline, especially since the Second World War when its numbers dwindled to alarmingly low levels. Happily it is now beginning to recover as many new fanciers are taking up the breeding of this famous old variety.

It is in this breed that the crest feature reaches the ultimate in size and development and, in general

terms, it can never be too large — provided always that its shape and formation are correct. It should consist of an abundance of broad, long and leafy feathers which radiate evenly all round from the small, neat centre of the crest well over the beak, eyes and back of the head. Birds with what are called *weeping* or *drooping* crests are always to be preferred to those with a flatter crest, although the latter are acceptable on the show bench so long as the crest is well filled and without any *splits* or *horns* and similar defects that can mar its appearance.

The ideal crest should be circular in form and any departures from this towards oval, ovate or shield shapes, although not a disqualification, naturally count against the bird in competition.

Aside from its crest, the Crested Canary is a stocky and well built bird which stands at a low angle across its perch. It tends to have an abundance of long feather about its body which generally necessitates a little trimming in the region of the vent before the breeding season so that successful fertilization is not impeded.

Official Standard

Unlike most other specialist societies, the Crested Canary Club of Great Britain does not issue a scale of points but merely relies upon a written standard describing the ideal bird. It reads as follows:

Size and formation of the crest shall be the first consideration. A crest cannot be too large. It should consist of an abundance of broad, long and veiny feathers, evenly radiated from a small centre, well over eyes, beak and poll. A good crest may be flat if well filled in at the back and without splits, but a drooping or weeping crest shall have preference. Type and quality are of next importance. The body should in shape resemble that of a bullfinch possessing substance in proportion to its length, with a broad back nicely arched, full and well circled chest, tail short and narrow, wings not extending beyond root of tail, nor crossed at tips, but fitting closely to the body. The neck should be full and the beak short. The bird should stand well across the perch on short legs, with thighs and hocks well set back. The Crest-bred should possess a body as above described. The head should be large and round, broad at every part, with a small beak and an abundance of long, broad feather commencing at entrance of beak, continuing over the crown and flowing well down the poll and should be well browed. In a good Crest-bred the feathers of the crown when turned over should reach the end of the beak and the heavy brows should give the bird a sulky appearance without brushing. When two or more birds are of equal merit in crest or head properties the smaller bird shall take precedence if of the correct type, the Club recognizing it to be the more difficult to obtain, but no restriction whatever is placed upon the length of the bird. Quality of feather and high condition to have due weight.

Objectionable properties
(1) Crest and Head — Crests shall not be horned at back, nor open at poll, nor split at sides or front; nor shall the centre be open or long, or too near the beak, back or sides; nor shall the crest be tilted, nor shall it consist of thin, scanty, hairy feather. The head of a Crest-bred shall not be narrow in any part, nor pinched over beak, nor shall it be flat, or covered with short scanty feather, or be rough or 'guttered'.
(2) Body — Crests and Crest-breds should not have long, thin, erect bodies with disproportionately long tails, should not be dipped in back or frilled on breast, or cross their wings at tips, or carry themselves in a curved or slovenly manner, or stand on long legs, and no show bird should possess such an amount of loose fluff or body feather as to make it difficult to make out its shape.

This breed of canary is also in favour on the continent of Europe. The *C.O.M.* has adapted the Crested Canary Club description to suit its own standard format and added a scale of points for the judging of Crests at shows over which it has jurisdiction.

Official Standard
The *C.O.M.* standard reads as follows:
HEAD — massive. The crest consists of broad leafy feathers radiating from a small neat centre, drooping well over beak and eyes. The crest cannot be too large

BREAST — full, well rounded
LEGS — short, thighs and hocks well set back
NECK — full and short
BACK — broad and nicely arched
WINGS — not to extend beyond root of tail, meeting at tips, lying close to body
TAIL — short and narrow
POSITION — the crest should stand at 45 degrees
BODY — should resemble the bullfinch
LENGTH — 16.5cm

All points being equal, a smaller bird shall take preference.

The scale of points is as follows:

	Points
CREST OR HEAD	45
BEAK	5
NECK	5
BODY (shape)	10
LEGS	5
PLUMAGE	10
POSITION	10
GENERAL CONDITION	10
	Total 100

CROSSBREEDING
The serious livestock breeder sees very little merit in crossbreeding. In certain species of farm stock, however (such as sheep and cattle) crossing is often undertaken deliberately with a view to producing a hardy and thrifty animal that will rapidly put on flesh and become a marketable commodity. The fate of such crossbreds, of course, ends at the slaughterhouse and they take no part in any further breeding programmes.

The canary breeder has no such justification for the practice and, even should he have no particular aspirations for the show bench, he would be well advised to confine his activities to the pure breeds. Crossbred or mongrel stock may be reasonably satisfactory if required merely as household pets, or as inmates of an ornamental aviary, but surplus birds of this kind will have no sale value whatever among fanciers.

It is, however, a curious fact that, in the past, certain of the now well-recognized breeds originated from deliberate crossbreeding. (See, for example, *GLOSTER FANCY CANARY, YORKSHIRE CANARY*.) Others of even more ancient date were improved and developed by means of selected and well-considered outcrosses. (See *CRESTED CANARY, NORWICH CANARY*).

Much more recently, efforts have been made to produce new breeds in this way. (See *AMERICAN SINGER, PADOVAN FRILL*.) In all of these cases, long periods of reselection and backcrossing have had to follow before the desired results are achieved and a genetically stable (i.e. true breeding) type becomes worthy of serious recognition as a genuine breed.

CUTTLEFISH BONE

Even those who keep only a single pet bird are familiar with this substance, and usually have a piece of it pushed between the wires of the cage or clipped into position with a special holder. The bony skeleton of the cuttlefish is made almost entirely of lime, and is a useful source of calcium at times when it is needed (such as in the breeding season to help the hens with the formation of egg-shells). Out of season its most useful function is most likely to be in providing solitary birds with some form of diversion and their constant nibbling at it helps to keep the beak worn down to some extent.

Cuttlefish bone can often be picked up on beaches but, because of the danger of pollution, it would always be advisable to scrape it clean of any surface deposits and to boil it well before use. The product offered for sale in pet shops and seed merchants would almost certainly have been so treated and therefore safe.

DEAD-IN-SHELL

It is not unusual for eggs to be a day later in hatching than expected (see *INCUBATION*) but, if the clutch becomes more than 48 hours overdue, it is almost certain that the chicks are dead in their shells. This unfortunate setback to the breeding season occurs when a fully developed, or almost fully developed embryo, dies at the point of hatching, or only a few hours before. Apparently, no scientific investigation has been carried out on the subject but fanciers tend to attribute the trouble to a variety of causes. Among these are such things as too dry an atmosphere at the crucial time of hatching and heavy thunderstorms overhead causing a disturbance to the sitting hens. There are several other possibilities also such as hereditary weakness, congenital defects, physical malformation and vitamin or mineral deficiency.

Whatever the cause, there is no remedy at the time and the breeding pair should be given a few days' rest before reconditioning and mating up again in, say, a week or ten days' time. It does occasionally happen, although very rarely, for a clutch to hatch three or four days late. Some fanciers will leave the hen to brood for this additional period before deciding to put an end to matters.

Avoidance of some of the possibilities mentioned above can clearly be achieved by:
1 Careful selection of healthy breeding stock, with a sound knowledge of their antecedents (i.e. no history of similar trouble among their ancestors);
2 Correct feeding, ensuring that there is no mineral or vitamin deficiency in their diet;
3 Making sure of a sufficiently

humid atmosphere in the birdroom by damping the floor, or providing a trough of water for evaporation.
(Thunderstorms, unfortunately, cannot be guarded against!)

It is reassuring to know, however, that the majority of canary fanciers are virtually untroubled by dead-in-shell.

DIET

Today we are well aware of the importance of diet. Through the media we are bombarded with facts about what is good and what is bad for us. It may come as a relief, therefore, to know that we are, in the main, feeding our canaries in much the same manner as did our forebears of a century ago.

Of course, much scientific research has gone into the highly commercial world of poultry keeping where the birds are fed on balanced diets according to their state of growth. These are usually in pelleted form and complete with the addition of antibiotics, etc. None of this has yet influenced the canary fancy, except for the occasional use of chick starter crumbs or turkey pellets. It may be that a complete canary feed may eventually become available that would take the guesswork out of feeding.

Traditional feeding still prevails and the canary's diet consists of:
1 A number of different kinds of seed;
2 Various types of greenfood;
3 Soft food, which may include egg food and/or bread and milk, according to the fancier's own preference.

Most of these items are dealt with at greater length under their appropriate headings.

A useful diet chart to follow for the basic winter feeding of breeding stock is as follows:
1 Staple seed mixture in the seed hoppers at all times, consisting of three parts of canary seed and one part of rape seed (or a general mixture of seeds as sold by fanciers' suppliers can be used if preferred);

2 Daily additions to this, given at the rate of one small teaspoonful per bird:
Sunday — soft food
Monday — greenfood
Tuesday — no extras
Wednesday — condition seed
Thursday — greenfood
Friday — no extras
Saturday — niger seed

Greenfood can consist of lettuce, cress, brussels sprouts, watercress, apple, carrot, etc.

DIMORPHIC

By definition, the word *dimorphic* simply means 'existing in two forms' but, in the canary fancy, it has a special significance by being applied to certain birds that exhibit *sexual dimorphism*. In many species of bird the differences between the sexes are very well marked but, in the canary generally, this is not so. It is quite difficult for even the experienced fancier to tell the difference between cocks and hens with certainty.

However, some years ago in the pioneer breeding of Red Factor Canaries, certain hens appeared which followed the plumage pattern of the Black-hooded Red Siskins (*Spinus cucullatus*) in their ancestry. In the clear form these hens are mainly off-white in colour, with some orange pigmentation on the wing butts, forehead and rump, and these are the birds that were called *dimorphics*.

More recently, another dimorphic mutation has arisen in which the cocks also show a distinctive plumage pattern. In the Red Canary these can be quite striking birds with their chalk-white body, red at the usual 'points' of rump and wing butts, but having also a characteristic red facial area somewhat reminiscent of the blaze of a Goldfinch. This gives the birds overall an almost startling red-and-white appearance.

These birds belong properly to the Coloured Canary section of the hobby. Standards governing their exhibition are as follows:

Dimorphic

All must show the requirements of dimorphism, i.e., only four colour points; face, shoulders, rump and chest. To be more specific, these areas are itemized further:

FACE — Hens to show 'eyebrows' only. Colour not to run from eye to eye nor down to cheeks. Cocks to show a blaze typical of a Goldfinch, i.e. an area of coloration extending centrally from the beak and should be as restricted as possible.

SHOULDERS — Small distinct area on shoulders only. Colour not to extend to wing flights.

RUMP — Small distinct area on top of rump, not to extend to back or under body.

CHEST — Slight area centrally on chest, not to flow up or down to head or under body. Remainder of body plumage, wings and tail to show bright clean white in clear varieties with corresponding colouring in self varieties. The colour points of the cocks will be enlarged in comparison to the hens.

FAULTS — (Hens particularly)

a Colouring above beak, on forehead, between beak and breast, running into wing flights;

b Rough feathering.

DISEASES

If the initial stock is healthy and is suitably housed and properly fed, disease rarely occurs. The fancier is advised to concentrate upon its prevention rather than its cure. With this in mind, the attitude towards disease should be:

1 Avoiding it by adopting sound methods of management;

2 Recognizing diseases at once, should they occur;

3 Applying the correct remedies for their treatment and control.

Among the preventive measures that can be taken is that of adopting sound breeding principles and refusing to breed with anything other than perfectly vigorous stock. There may be the temptation at times to overlook a slight defect in the health of an outstanding show bird in the hope of breeding a few sound youngsters. However, such a course could lead to an eventual deterioration in the stamina of a strain, especially if inbreeding is practised.

The importance of a balanced diet is also well recognized and so not only should the correct foods be given, and in the correct proportions, but care must also be taken to ensure that the quality is good, with freedom from any staleness or contamination. Greenfood in particular should be obtained from sources known to be free from agricultural sprays or fouling by domestic animals. Any food of a soft, or green, nature that has remained unconsumed should be removed from the cages not later than the following day. Feeding and drinking vessels also should be regularly washed and disinfected.

The importance of clean, airy, draught-free and damp-proof quarters is discussed under the heading *BIRDROOMS* and the routine cleaning and disinfecting of cages under *MANAGEMENT* but even when these are strictly followed situations may still arise which could nullify all the care previously taken. It is therefore always advisable to be alert for any possible sources of infection and to be scrupulous on points of hygiene.

If, at any time, a bird should happen to become sick a certain basic course of action should be followed:

1 If it has been housed with others, it should be taken away and caged on its own — preferably in a hospital cage;

2 As soon as possible, clean out and disinfect the cage it was occupying in case the complaint is infectious.

3 Keep on a plain diet (seed only) and administer a mild aperient (purgative) in the drinking water for a day or so.

Apart from a few of the more obvious cases, it is extremely difficult to diagnose most of the diseases in canaries. Those with larger stocks of birds at risk, however, usually consult a veterinary surgeon and good results usually follow the use of a course of antibiotics.

DISINFECTION

As outlined in the previous section, the routine cleansing and disinfection of cages is a sensible precaution in the prevention of disease. At the weekly cleaning-out time, wiping down the walls and wires of the cages with a damp cloth that has been dipped in a suitable disinfectant should be adequate but, both before and after the breeding season, the cages should be taken outside and thoroughly washed out.

Care must be exercised in using any kind of disinfectant which should always be diluted to the strengths recommended by the manufacturers. The perches should be well rinsed in clean water afterwards and dried before being replaced. Birds have the habit of frequently wiping their beaks upon the perches and sore faces as well as sore feet could arise if a strong deposit of disinfectant was left upon them.

The birdroom itself can also, with advantage, be thoroughly disinfected in the spring before the start of the breeding season so that everything is clean and fresh before this important phase of the hobby begins. Occasionally it may be thought desirable to fumigate the birdroom in its entirety, particularly if the fancier has been unlucky enough to have a contagious disease among his stock or, indeed, an infestation of certain parasites. In this case good results have been achieved by the use of formaldehyde vapour which is produced by pouring a solution of formalin upon crystals of permanganate of potash. It would be necessary to remove all birds from the room while the operation takes place. Then, after sealing the windows and ventilators, the permanganate crystals should be placed in a metal container on the floor and the formalin poured over them. The door should be then closed and the room left for 12 hours, after which the vapour should be allowed to disperse and the birdroom well ventilated before the birds are returned.

This method is very effective against most insect pests and other organisms such as bacteria and fungi but, of course, cannot deal with anything that may be on the birds themselves. The use of smoke or vapour generators such as are used in the fumigation of greenhouses should not be contemplated; these may be based upon chemicals that could prove harmful to the birds when they are returned.

Although all of these precautions will not necessarily guarantee a good breeding season, they will at least play some part in contributing to success by elminating some of the possible causes of failure.

DOMINANT WHITE

White canaries are to be found in most of the popular breeds and many fanciers keep a few. This presents no great difficulty, since the Whites are required to be bred to the same standard of the breed whether it be Border, Gloster, Norwich, Yorkshire, etc.

There are two different kinds of white Canaries in existence. They arose from quite separate and distinct mutations, known as *dominant* and *recessive* whites according to their mode of inheritance. Practically all of the white birds found in the type breeds are of the dominant kind, whereas the recessive Whites are more widely kept in Coloured Canary circles.

Like the crest mutation, the dominant white is another example of a lethal effect being induced when the gene responsible is present in both chromosome pairs. The usual mating to apply, therefore, is White x normal. It is immaterial which partner is the cock and which is the hen. The progeny from such a mating will average out at 50% White and 50% normal. White x White can be used as a mating but it will still produce a proportion (25%) of normal

Yellow ground youngsters as well as having some non-viable progeny.

DRINKERS
This is the term for a whole range of receptacles used for supplying birds with water. Throughout the history of the fancy designs for these have varied, ranging from the somewhat ornamental ones often favoured by the Victorians, to the plainly utilitarian ones in use today. The ones that are most commonly in use are called *glass hat* drinkers although they are quite often now made in clear plastic. Their advantage is that they are nicely rounded off and smooth on the inside, like a wine glass, with no angles or corners to harbour dirt or encourage the growth of algae.

The D-shaped show cage drinkers of the two-hook type, as used in Norwich, Lizard, Gloster, etc., show cages, are not suitable for daily use. It is very easy when in continual use for the angles of a drinker to become the habitat of green algae.

Fountains — plastic tubular clip-on drinkers, have some advantages in that seed husks, sawdust and dirt cannot get into them, but they are a little more trouble to replenish and clean out than the standard hat type.

DUMMY EGGS
It usually comes as a surprise to any newcomer to the fancy to learn that he needs a supply of dummy eggs. It is the usual practice to remove the canary's real eggs from the nest as they are laid and to replace them with dummies until she has completed her clutch and is ready to begin incubating. At this stage the dummies are all taken away and the real eggs replaced; the idea is that they will all hatch out at almost the same time and thus the chicks will have an equal start in life and continue at an even growth rate. Dummy eggs, usually made of plastic, are available from the usual fanciers' suppliers of accessories.

EGGS
For those who have never had any previous experience, it is always a moment of great excitement to get one's first eggs of the season, for therein lies so much hope and expectation. Even the old hands, if they were to admit it, get the same thrill each year at the start of the breeding season. The canary's egg follows very much the general pattern of the finch family, having a pale greenish-blue background and being spotted with reddish brown, not very densely and more towards the larger end. An interesting variation that sometimes occurs is among Frilled Canaries where some of the hens are prone to laying pure white eggs.

The normal clutch for a canary consists of four or five eggs; it is the usual practice to remove each egg as laid and replace it with a dummy until the clutch is complete. (See *DUMMY EGGS*.)

Eggs are very fragile and easily broken, thus it is a good idea always to move them with a teaspoon. A safe place in which to store them until ready for incubation is essential and, for this

Clutch of canary's eggs showing typical markings

purpose, most fanciers have an *egg box*. This is merely a shallow box, or tray of some kind, divided into compartments of about 5 to 8cm (2 to 3in) square corresponding to the number of breeding cages being used, and numbered accordingly. Each section should be partly filled with some soft material, such as fine sawdust or cotton wool, so that the eggs will remain safe until ready for replacement. There is no need to keep them in a warm place, nor to turn them daily; they should be left alone until the clutch is complete.

If the breeding hens are in proper condition at the time of mating, the first egg will probably be laid within a week or ten days. During this period the pair will have been nest building, sometimes with a certain amount of lack of purpose to begin with, but when the nest is obviously finished and the hen tends to roost alongside it, or even in it, at night, she may be expected to lay fairly soon. She will drink an increased amount of water for a period of about 48 hours before the event.

Eggs are normally laid early in the morning, before about 7.30 am, and fanciers who attend to their birds at this time of day may often see the hens in the act of laying. Needless to say no hen should ever be disturbed at this time; wait until she leaves the nest to feed and then take away the nest for a moment, remove the egg, replace it with a dummy one and then return the nest to its place in the breeding cage.

The eggs are usually laid at 24-hour intervals so that the clutch will be complete on the fourth morning when all the real eggs can be returned for incubation. It does not matter if a fifth one is subsequently laid; the late-hatched chick will have to take its chance and usually survives. Occasionally a hen will miss a day in the laying sequence but there is no cause for alarm. If, however, a couple of days go by without further eggs it is likely that the hen has finished laying and there is going to be a smaller clutch than normal.

EGG BINDING

This can cause the fancier a good deal of anxiety. It can be defined as a condition in which a hen is unable to expel the egg from the oviduct. In mild cases it may do nothing more than cause her slight distress for a while until the egg has been passed, but in severe cases she can become prostrated and in a complete state of collapse through exhaustion.

The symptoms of egg binding are easily recognized. The hen will be found in the nest, on the floor of the cage, or sitting on the perch, huddled up with eyes half closed and feathers puffed out, and making periodic straining movements in an effort to expel the egg.

The best form of immediate treatment is to remove the sufferer to a really warm place such as a hospital cage, if one is available, or a small cage placed near a fire or radiator. It will often be found that this alone is sufficient to bring relief.

If after an hour or so the egg still has not been passed, a little warm olive oil can be dropped into the vent to act as a lubricant but it is wise never to attempt to remove the egg manually.

Hens can certainly be lost through egg binding, but most of them make a recovery and, after a few hours, act as though nothing untoward had happened. A really bad case will always leave the bird somewhat weakened and may render her useless for the remainder of the season. By way of reassurance it must be said finally that egg binding rarely occurs at all if hens are of sound, healthy stock and have been properly managed throughout the winter months. This means giving them a plain but adequate diet, plenty of fresh air and ample exercise so that they are fully fit and in hard condition at the beginning of the breeding season.

EGG FOOD

This forms one of the most important items for the rearing of young canaries, along with soaked seed, wild seeds and greenstuff. In former times fanciers made their own, usually by blending a hard-boiled egg, that had been passed through a kitchen sieve, with crushed biscuits. No doubt millions of canaries were satisfactorily reared in this way but, since those days, many other recipes have been developed. Although some fanciers still prefer to prepare their own egg food, probably many more now make use of the various proprietary brands of rearing food on the market.

If it is preferred to make one's own, various blendings of wholemeal bread, fine oatmeal and one of the well-known baby cereal foods (which will take care of the vitamin and mineral content) should be used. A small sprinkling of caster sugar and maw seed can be added to make the mixture attractive to the birds. The bread should be cut into thin slices or fingers, dried in a slow oven and then put through a mincer. It can be thoroughly blended with the other ingredients and stored until required for use. Small quantities only should be prepared at a time in order to prevent staleness. This basic dry mixture will merely need moistening to a crumbly moist consistency before blending with the egg which, as stated, should have been boiled for about 10 minutes and then pressed through a sieve. The proportions should be about one large breakfast cupful of the mixture to one hard-boiled egg.

Although it may be quite satisfying to make one's own rearing food, it is time-consuming and the busy fancier will usually turn to one of the many preparations that are on the market and feed according to the maker's directions.

Egg food is usually offered to the breeding pairs in egg food drawers — small plastic or earthenware receptacles designed to fit firmly under the door of the cage. It should be given fresh two or three times daily and no unconsumed egg food should be left in the drawers when new food is provided as deterioration can be fairly rapid in hot summer weather.

EVEN-MARKED

In the past, evenly marked canaries were very much admired by fanciers, to the extent that separate classes were provided for them at shows, as distinct from the ordinary run of irregularly marked, or variegated specimens. They are certainly most attractive, and still much to be admired, although now no particular importance is

Evenly marked bird with the six technical markings

attached to them, type always being the major consideration.

In these birds the markings are limited to three areas of the body only, namely the eyes, the secondary flight feathers and the outer tail feathers. They are recognized by special terms which, in some circles, are designated as technical markings as follows:

1 SIX POINTED An evenly marked specimen in which all six marks are present, i.e., touching each eye, both wings and each side of the tail.
2 FOUR POINTED A bird possessing four of the technical marks in any even combination, as for example, both eyes and both wings, both wings and outer tail feathers, or both eyes and outer tail feathers. Of these, the birds most usually seen are the ones with eye and wing markings.
3 TWO POINTED A bird having only two technical marks, which again must be symmetrical. These are usually the two wing marks.

As stated previously, evenly marked birds now take their place among the classes for variegated birds on the show bench. Care should be taken, however, when entering Yorkshire Canaries as this section of the fancy still makes use of technical markings in their classification, where their definitions sometimes differ from the more widely accepted ones.

EXHIBITING

After passing through the successive phases of weaning, moulting and training, it is the show season that becomes the ultimate objective of the canary fancier — or at least it should do. (See also *SHOWING*.)

The continued development and perfecting of the exhibition types of canary thrives upon the competition afforded by the show bench and it surely gives only comparatively minor satisfaction to a fancier to have a room full of excellent canaries if nobody else has the chance of seeing them. Every true fancier therefore almost has a duty to exhibit his birds at the appropriate season. Also, it is the only real measure of his progress to compare his own birds side by side with those of others and to submit them to the independent opinion of the judges.

The practical aspects of show training and procedure are dealt with under the letter **S**.

EXHIBITIONS (TYPES OF)

Every week throughout the show season, which varies from country to country, dozens of shows are being held. They may range from relatively small local events up to the large national and international exhibitions that are held in many countries. The newcomer to the fancy will need to know something of the nature of the competition that may be encountered in the various recognized categories. In Great Britain, the following types of show are in operation:

1 ANNUAL MEMBERS' SHOWS Entries to these shows are confined to members of the society only and no outsider can exhibit. Often there is only a nominal qualifying period of perhaps a fortnight for a newly-joined member before he becomes eligible to compete. In small societies the number of birds exhibited may be fairly limited, perhaps three or four hundred only, but in the case of flourishing societies in large population centres there may well be a thousand or more. In addition to their main annual show, many local clubs stage a pairs show and a young stock show. These can prove instructive for the beginner.

2 OPEN SHOWS These are promoted and organized by various local cage bird societies, either instead of, or in addition to, their own members' annual fixture. In these, entries are accepted from fanciers anywhere in the country without membership being a condition for participation. This is the meaning of 'open', i.e. entry is open to anybody, and so in general, the competition is likely to be much more searching than at local level. Most of the better open shows have entries of between 1500 and 2000 birds, although not all of them are necessarily as popular as this. The large national shows previously referred to also fall into the open category and may have entries three or four times the numbers quoted above.

3 SPECIALIST SOCIETIES' SHOWS Canary specialist societies exist in some countries which cater for those enthusiasts who keep one variety only (e.g., the Border Fancy Canary Club, the Crested Canary Club, the Lizard Canary Association, and so on). Some of these may be large enough and with sufficient financial backing, to be able to stage their own shows in which only their breed is exhibited. The majority, however, have a working agreement with certain open show promoting societies that is known as *patronage*. In this way, when patronage is granted, a specialist society's members agree to support that particular show with their entries

(Photographed by Cage and Aviary)

Exhibition of canaries staged in a well lit show hall

F

so that a good classification for their own breed can be offered. This arrangement benefits both the specialist society, which is thus spared the expense of staging its own show, and the show promoting society, which thereby gains additional entries. Usually at a patronage show some of the specialist society's trophies, plus cash inducements, are offered for competition in order to boost the entries.

EYES

The colour of the eye in normally pigmented birds is black but in the case of Cinnamon Canaries it is usually referred to as being pink. Most text books on canaries refer to Cinnamons as pink-eyed birds. Actually it is more of a plum colour and is only readily distinguishable in nestlings; as the bird grows older the eye colour becomes much darker until it is difficult to differentiate from the normal. (See *CINNAMON*.)

More recent mutations have produced canaries which have red eyes which, unlike the pink eye of the Cinnamon, do not alter in adulthood so that there are now canaries on the show bench with quite startling ruby red eyes. These are to be found in the *Ino* and *Satinette* series of Coloured Canaries. (See relevant headings.)

FEATHERS

Aside from the two basic feather types to be found in canaries (see *BUFF* and *YELLOW*), fanciers occasionally need to refer to specific feathers. Most basic books on ornithology have an outline diagram of a bird with its external features indicated, starting with the mandibles and ending with the tail. Clearly these terms could be useful when discussing points with a fellow fancier but, in practice, few are used in normal conversation. Apart from the *flight feathers* of the wings and tail, perhaps the *wing coverts* and the *upper* and *lower tail coverts* are the only ones that may be necessary. Such obvious features as the rump, shoulders, back, throat and thighs are self explanatory and accurate enough for most purposes.

Feathers are structures peculiar to birds and are presumed to have evolved from the scaly covering of their primitive reptile-like ancestors. The canary fancier recognizes two kinds of feather in his birds: the contour feathers which clothe, protect and insulate the body, and the flight and tail feathers which are concerned with the process of flying. The former vary considerably in size, ranging from the tiny feathers on the head to the large, broad ones on the back, breast and flanks. The same variation is not to be seen in the flying feathers although the primaries are longer than the secondaries.

The wing covert feathers are intermediate in form between these two types. The greater coverts protect the base of the flight feathers and the lesser coverts insulate and protect the fleshy part of the wing from which the flights are growing.

All feathers have the same basic

structure consisting of a quill, or shaft, and the web, or vane, which spreads out on either side of the shaft. It is by this shaft that the feather is attached to the skin and through which it receives nourishment during the course of its growth.

The feathers develop from tiny papillae on the skin and grow in orderly lines on certain areas of the body known as feather tracts which can clearly be seen in a nestling.

The growing feather follicles draw their nourishment from the bloodstream through a small opening at their base but when the feather is fully expanded this is sealed off and the feather becomes a dead structure. No further growth will take place unless a feather is lost in which case a new one will grow in its place. Canaries renew their covering of feathers annually. (See *MOULTING*.)

FEATHER PLUCKING

This vice is known to exist in all branches of birdkeeping, ranging from parrots to poultry, and including, of course, canaries. Fortunately, it is not a common occurrence in adult stock if proper measures are taken in its avoidance.

Self plucking almost never occurs, except in the case of some hens that are ready and eager to nest and have no nesting material. The remedy here is obvious: provide them with some nesting material to keep them happy and take heed of the signs by getting them paired up as soon as possible and a nest pan introduced. Some fanciers will also tie a piece of string to the wires of the cage for the hen to pull at, and this remedy is generally successful as in other cases of feather plucking.

Occasionally, hens wanting to go to nest for the second time will turn to plucking their own first brood of youngsters, if these have not already been weaned, and so a sharp lookout should be kept at this period of the breeding cycle. If suspected the course of action to take is to separate the adult pair from their offspring by means of a wire sliding partition. They can then continue to feed them through the bars and yet be unable to denude them of feathers.

The final danger of plucking occurs among the young birds in their flight cages before their first moult begins. Like all young creatures they are active, inquisitive, and need plenty to occupy their attention, otherwise they will get into mischief. Overcrowding is the worst possible condition conducive to plucking and a lot of youngsters can be spoiled through lack of awareness of the problem. They should be given ample flying space and plenty to peck at in the way of seeding weeds and grasses, plus some string tied to the wires of their cage, as mentioned above.

If, in spite of this, plucking does occur, it will be necessary to spend a little time in watching the birds in order to detect the culprit (for it often starts with only one) who should then be caught up and caged on its own before the vice spreads to others. Birds that have been plucked will have feathers missing from the lower part of their backs, in serious cases becoming quite denuded in this area with the skin raw and sore. This attracts the attention of other canaries who continue the attacks. The victim should be separated from its companions until the feathers have grown again.

In most cases no lasting damage is done but in Lizard Canaries plucking must be avoided at all costs since, in this breed, the plumage is all important and a bird could have its entire show career ruined. Lizard breeders, therefore, often cage their entire show stock separately. (See *LIZARD CANARY*.)

FEATHER QUALITY

Quality of feather is readily pointed out and recognized but less easily defined in words. Most dictionaries refer to quality as 'a degree of excellence', 'distinctive in character', and so on. However, in the canary world, if a bird has sleek, closely fitting plumage, with well braced wings, a tightly folded tail and no looseness at the waist and/or thighs, it is generally held to be of good feather quality. This condition is a most desirable one in the majority of breeds, and readily achieved in the smaller ones such as Fifes and Lizards. In some of the larger breeds it is more difficult to attain because, so often, size or length of body is gained by means of a profusion of feathering.

In certain other varieties feather quality, in the accepted sense, is conspicuously lacking and here reference should be made to such breeds as Frills, Lancashires and Crests. In the case of the former, length and density of feather is a desirable characteristic while, in the two crested breeds, length of body feather is a necessary adjunct to obtaining large crests on their heads. It follows, therefore, that the quality of feather that is right for these breeds is different from the feather quality as generally understood by the rest of the fancy.

FEEDERS

This term is used in the fancy for birds that are used as foster parents. Quite a number of fanciers make use of them for a variety of reasons, most common of which is a form of safety resource to ensure that, if anything goes wrong with the rearing of their exhibition youngsters, the feeders can take over the task. This sounds to be a sensible precaution but it does not always work out so simply in practice. The general idea is that, at breeding time, a number of well-tried and trusted birds are paired up (often common songsters, or crossbreds) at the same time as the show stock so that they will be on hand to take over the responsibilities of rearing if required. Some fanciers start by putting the eggs of their high-class birds under the feeding hens at the outset, but many have tales to tell of their feeders letting the youngsters die while the show hens have safely reared the mongrels!

Although there will always be exceptional circumstances, it is generally advisable to have nothing at all to do with feeders but to concentrate upon the production of a good exhibition self-feeding strain of birds.

FERTILITY

Obviously, fertility is of the utmost importance in the breeding season for nothing is more disappointing, after a promising start has been made, than to get what fanciers call *clear* eggs. Few, if any, birds are genetically infertile and so it is largely a matter of ensuring that they are fully fit before embarking upon the breeding programme. This is generally achieved by a gradual build-up in the diet as the breeding season approaches, with special care in ensuring that the full range of vitamins and minerals is available.

Fanciers who are in a position to do so, should make use of the great variety of natural foods such as wild plants and seeding weeds commonly consumed by native finches and various kinds of greenstuff from the garden. Town dwellers can always obtain cress, lettuce, watercress, chicory and so on from the greengrocer. (The use of *CONDITION SEED* has already received mention under that heading.)

Food supplements are readily available from fanciers' suppliers in the form of mineralized grit or complete mineral and vitamin supplements, many of which are advertised in the fancy press. Some vitamins are soluble and are merely added to the birds' drinking water, while others are in powder form and need to be incorporated in the soft food. The so-called fertility vitamin (Vitamin E) is present in wheat-germ oil. This is readily obtainable and can be added to the seed mixture at the rate of one teaspoonful of the oil to one pound of seed — some time being allowed for the oil to become absorbed.

It should here be emphasized that by no means all of these additives need be employed. Vitamins and minerals are needed by the body in almost infinitessimal amounts and if a well balanced diet with plenty of fresh food is normally given, they may not be needed at all.

One further occasional cause of infertility is a purely physical one. Heavily feathered canaries, such as the Frilled or Crested varieties, possess such a density of feather in the region of the vent, that effective contact during copulation is sometimes prevented. Breeders of these varieties will, therefore, usually trim the feathers of the tail coverts and those around the vent and thighs to a more normal length before putting their breeding pairs together.

(see colour feature page 94)

FIFE FANCY

Some enthusiasts have attempted to popularize miniaturized versions of certain standard breeds — with conspicuous lack of success except in the case of the Fife Fancy. This is, in effect, a scaled down version of the *BORDER FANCY* (which see), although not presenting quite the same contrast in size to the parent breed as bantams do to the standard fowl.

The early enthusiasts of this delightful little canary founded their first specialist society in 1957 at Kirkaldy in Fife, Scotland, from which circumstance the breed takes its name. At first, interest was largely local and progress relatively slow. More recently the breed has been receiving the attention it deserves and Fifes are now to be found throughout the British Isles. They have also found their way onto the continent of Europe and to other parts of the world.

The Fife Fancy has descended directly from the Border itself with probably no other canary being used. The early type of Border was a very much smaller bird than it is today. As larger and larger birds began to find favour with fanciers, there were clearly some who were not at all enamoured with the trend and still continued to breed the smaller version. Eventually the gap between the two was sufficiently great for the new breed to be distinct and recognizable. The fancy is now fortunate in having a really charming little canary.

Since the Fife is virtually a miniature version of the Border, much of what has been written about that breed is equally applicable here. The sole exception is its size which the breed society states should not exceed 11cm (4.5in). Its tiny size, perky manner

Official Standard

The standard and scale of points for the Fife Fancy Canary are as follows:

Points

HEAD — Small, round and neat — beak fine; eyes central to roundness of head and body	10
BODY — Well filled and nicely rounded running in almost a straight line from the gentle rise over the shoulders to the point of the tail, chest also rounded, but neither heavy nor prominent	10
WINGS — Compact and carried close to the body, meeting at the tips, just below root of tail	10
LEGS — Of medium length, showing little thigh	5
PLUMAGE — Close, firm, fine in quality	10
TAIL — Close packed and narrow being nicely rounded and filled in at the root	5
POSITION AND CARRIAGE — Semi-erect, standing at an angle of 60 degrees. Gay, jaunty, with full poise of head	10
COLOUR — Rich, soft and pure, as level in tint as possible throughout, but extreme depth and hardness such as colour feeding gives are debarred	10
HEALTH — Condition and cleanliness shall have due weight	5
SIZE — Not to exceed 4¼in	25
	Total 100

and confiding nature are all attributes which enhance its finely balanced proportions and superb feather quality. These, plus its free-breeding propensities, make it a breed above all others that is well suited to the needs of the beginner in canary culture.

Fifes are now being exhibited in the original Dewar cage that was designed, and is still used, for the Border although moves are afoot to have a separate and distinctive cage adopted that will be more in keeping with the bird's tiny size and accepted status as a new breed.

FLIGHTS
The term *flights* can have different uses. It can be used to mean flight feathers (the large flying feathers in the wing of the bird); or flight cages (the specially long stock cages that afford extra exercise and flying distance for the birds that are housed therein). The small aviaries attached to a birdroom to give either indoor, or outdoor accommodation for larger numbers of birds than would otherwise be the case, are also often called flights.

When in conversation with fellow fanciers it is obvious that no confusion as to meaning need ever arise since the word will be appreciated according to the context in which it is being used.

FLUE
This word, in its full form of *underflue*, has already received passing mention under an earlier heading when discussing the definition of a clear bird. It is the soft, fluffy part of a feather between the web, which shows on the surface, and the bird's skin. Taken in its entirety the flue forms a dense and downy layer providing the bird with an effective form of insulation. The web of the feather forms an outer coat which traps the warmth within and sheds off water; it is kept in good condition by the bird during preening.

The colour of the underflue can be of some help in identifying many

of the newer mutations. It may be brown, beige, slate, silver grey and so on but, in the ordinary clear canary it is white, and in greens it is a very dark grey, in fact almost black.

FOUL (FOUL FEATHERS, or FOUL MARKED)
This is one of the recognized terms used in the *CLASSIFICATION* (which see) of canaries. It does not, of course, imply being offensive or dirty but irregular or imperfect. It is applied to dark plumaged birds, such as greens or cinnamons, which may have some white feathers among the flight feathers

of their wings or in their tails. There is no universal ruling on just how many white feathers are allowed; three is sometimes quoted, but some authorities will accept any number so long as there are no other light feathers

Foul marked Crested Canary showing white feathers in the tail

Crested Canary that is three-parts dark with light feathering elsewhere on the body

48

anywhere else on the body. In practice, the presence of a largish number of white feathers in the wings or tail is very often accompanied by areas of light feathering elsewhere, usually under the chin or in the area of the vent. For this reason, some specialist societies, notably those of the Border and Gloster, recognize an additional category in the classification which they designate *three-parts dark*.

In Lizard Canaries the words *foul-tailed* or *foul-winged* are used to describe those particular faults which are so serious in this breed as to render the bird unfit for competition.

(see colour feature pages 122-123, 127)

FRILLED CANARIES

The frill is one of the few examples of a mutation that affects the formation and unusual disposition of the feathers. This mutation is said to have occurred in Holland about the year 1800. During the nineteenth century, canaries possessing the characteristic gradually spread throughout Europe. They were then known as Dutch Canaries until such time as local varieties were developed and were sufficiently recognizable to warrant separate names.

For some reason, however, they never became popular in Britain and did not even merit a mention by the eminent Victorian writers on canaries, many of whom compiled quite comprehensive books on the subject. Around the turn of the century, some writers did give space to them but, so little were they understood, that whatever their type, they were always referred to as Dutch Frills.

The crest mutation, it will be recalled, gave rise to a particular arrangement of feathers upon the crown of the head, but in the case of the frills, there are three areas of the body where specific forms of feathering occur and each one is recognized by a distinctive name.

1 The feathers on the back are divided by a central parting running longitudinally from between the shoulders to the lower back. From this the frilled nature of the plumage results in the feathers curling forward over the shoulders and wings, evenly on each side, rather like a cape. This feature is called the *mantle*.

2 The breast feathers, instead of running smoothly down the length of the body in the normal way, curl forwards and upwards over the breastbone and towards the throat to form a kind of frilly shirt-front which is known as the *jabot* (or sometimes *craw* in Britain).

3 A sizeable bunch of feathers on the flanks, just above each thigh, curls outwards and upwards in a sweeping fashion concentrically around the wings. These frills are called the *fins*.

All frilled breeds of the canary possess this basic arrangement of the feathers and any additional frilling, or lack of it, coupled with the attitude or posture of the bird plus its size, distinguishes between the various breeds.

The full list of Frilled breeds at present recognized by the *Confederation Ornithologique Mondiale* is as follows: the *NORTH DUTCH FRILL*, the *SOUTH DUTCH FRILL* (also somewhat confusingly known as the French Frill), the *PARISIAN FRILL*, the *MILAN FRILL*, the *SWISS FRILL*, *GIBBER ITALICUS* and *GIBBOSO ESPAGNOLE*. They are all quite fascinating birds of a very ornamental appearance and will be dealt with in further detail under their individual titles.

FRONTAL

This is a technical term, used by the breeders of crested varieties, which refers to the forward part of the crest above the beak. The frontal should consist of long and broad feathers which reach the end of the beak, or even beyond it, drooping evenly and without any split in the outline above the upper mandible. A really good frontal is much to be desired and is equally quite difficult to achieve, many crested birds being far too short in front.

Lizard

Examples of Lizard Canaries:

Top: Broken Capped Gold

Right: Non-capped Silver

Far right: Broken Capped Silver

Lizard Canaries
from Cassell's
"Book of Canaries
and Cage-Birds"

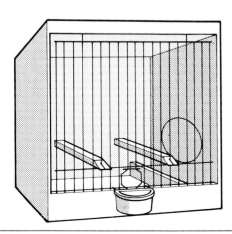

Show cage
designed by the
Lizard Canary
Association of
Great Britain

Player's Cigarettes

Lizard Canary

G

GENETICS

Elsewhere in this book occasional references have been made to the science of genetics which has helped us to understand the interrelationship of certain characteristics in the canary. Examples of this have been Green and Cinnamon, Crest and Plainhead and Yellow and Buff.

Practical fanciers have probably got along without any knowledge of genetics quite well for the past couple of hundred years and doubtless will continue to do so. Nevertheless it is an interesting subject which some may find useful, in its simpler aspects, to aid them in their hobby. A brief outline is given here.

First it must be understood that the body cells of every living organism contain two sets of chromosomes, consisting of matched pairs which have been inherited one from each parent. The reproductive cells, however (i.e., male sperm and female ovum in the case of the canary) contain only one set of chromosomes for the obvious reason that, when they meet in the act of fertilization, the sets can pair off and so become functional for the start of a new life.

Upon these chromosomes are to be found many genes which are complex chemical structures that, in association with environmental factors, control the entire development of the new individual. Each gene, working with its partner, determines how this individual shall develop.

Sometimes a balance is struck between the two so that a characteristic will be intermediate in form between the two parental types. Sometimes one has more influence than the other, thus producing in the offspring a leaning towards the features of one parent. Most of the purely physical characteristics such as shape of head, length of neck, quality of feather, carriage of body, and so on, fall into one of these two categories.

There are other examples, however, where one gene may be completely dominant to its partner, thus supressing the development of the characteristic involved altogether. It is this phenomenon of dominance and recessiveness that is of special interest to the breeder.

The first scientific experiments into the subject were carried out by Gregor Mendel (1822-84), using plant material. By means of hand-pollination he crossed two contrasting strains of garden peas; one grew very tall and the other was a dwarf variety. The outcome of this cross was that all of the succeeding generation (the 'F_1' in genetical terms) when grown on, proved to be tall like one of the parents; in other words dwarfness was a recessive characteristic. This was proved by self-pollination of the hybrid tall peas which, in the next generation (the 'F_2'), caused dwarf peas to re-emerge.

When the numbers of these were analysed mathematically, it was found to be a remarkably consistent 25%. Further experiments substantiated this which eventually led to the appreciation of what was happening. This can be shown diagrammatically as follows:

1 Tall peas (T) crossed with dwarf peas (d):

Genetic make-up	
Reproductive cells	
F_1 generation	

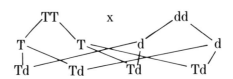

Results

All the plants are tall since tallness is dominant over dwarfness; but note that they are 'carrying' the gene for dwarfness, which can reappear as follows:

2 Hybrid Tall (Td) crossed with Hybrid Tall (Td):

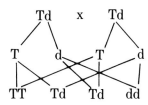

Results

25% pure breeding tall plants (TT),
50% hybrid tall plants (Td) and 25% dwarf (dd).

3 Hybrid Tall (Td) crossed with Dwarf (dd):

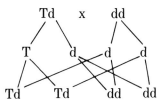

Results

50% hybrid tall (Td) and 50% dwarf (dd).

Mendelian Inheritance in Canaries

The hybrid types are now called heterozygous and the pure breeding types homozygous. In the third example quoted, there is the typical mode of inheritance when a heterozygous dominant is crossed with a homozygous recessive, i.e., 50% of each type among the progeny. This is a common expectation in certain characteristics in the canary as, for example, the usual mating of the two feather types, Yellow and Buff. In this it is the Yellow that is the heterozygous dominant

characteristic, Buff being the homozygous recessive, so that the mating is explained as follows:

4 Yellow (Yb) mated to Buff (bb):

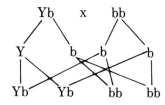

Results

50% Yellows (Yb) and 50% Buffs (bb).

It must be realized that the mathematical predictions of genetics are accurate over a large sample of progeny only. Mendel raised hundreds of plants to count in order to verify his results and substantiate his theory. In the canary, where probably a maximum of eight young may be produced in one year from any given pair of birds, the 50-50 prediction might not be manifest. The pairing of sperm with ovum is a random affair that might be compared with the tossing of a coin where, if a hundred or so throws were made, the result would be approximately half heads and half tails, whereas a small number of throws (say eight) could quite easily all be heads, or seven heads and one tail. Thus it is possible, although unlikely, for a normal pair of canaries, consisting of one Yellow and one Buff, to produce all Buff youngsters in one season but, if they could be kept together long enough to produce 100 young, the accuracy of the genetical forecast would become apparent.

Crest and Plainhead is another example of a heterozygous dominant (the Crest) and a homozygous recessive (the Plainhead) producing 50% of each type among the progeny. In this case there is an added factor to note insofar as the crest gene, if present on both chromosomes, has a lethal effect and renders the inheritor non-viable:

Mules

Above: Linnet-Canary Mule

Left: Greenfinch-Canary Mule

Below: Bullfinch-Canary Mule

Goldfinch-Canary Mules as illustrated in Cassell's "Book of Canaries and Cage-Birds". The evenly marked example is still extremely difficult to produce

Player's Cigarettes

Goldfinch-Canary Mule

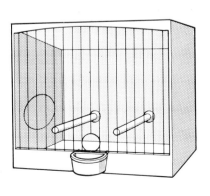

Player's Cigarettes

Bullfinch-Canary Mule

Type of cage in which Mules are shown in Great Britain

5 Normal mating of Crest (Cp) to Plainhead (pp):

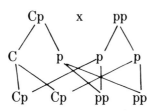

Results
50% crests (Cp) and 50% plainheads (pp).

6 The mating of two Crests together (both Cp):

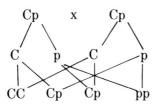

Results
25% non-viable Crests (CC), 50% normal Crests (Cp) and 25% Plainheads.

Note should also be taken of the fact that two Plainheads mated together can only produce plain-headed progeny, even though they themselves may have been bred from a Crest x Crest mating.

The inheritance of the Dominant White factor is the same as that of the crest and it, too, is lethal in the double dose.

7 The mating of Dominant White (Wn) to a normal canary (nn):

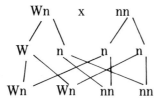

Results
50% Dominant Whites (Wn) and 50% normals (nn).

8 Dominant White (Wn) mated to another Dominant White (Wn):

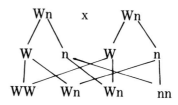

Results
25% non-viable Whites (WW), 50% Dominant Whites (Wn) and 25% normals (nn).

The Recessive White, however, has a different mode of inheritance as follows:

9 Normal canary (NN) mated to a Recessive White (ww):
(Note that the symbols NN are here in capitals as in this case it is the dominant characteristic.)

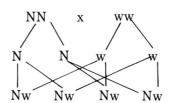

Results
All normals (Nw) but, like Mendel's tall hybrid peas, they are carrying the recessive (white) gene and can reproduce it in the following manner:

10 Normal, carrying recessive white (Nw) mated to another Normal, carrying Recessive White (Nw):

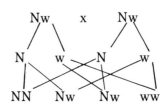

Results

25% normal canaries (NN), 50% normals, carrying recessive white (Nw) and 25% Recessive Whites (ww). It should also be noted that the 75% of birds that are normal in appearance can only be distinguished genetically by their breeding performance.

Sex-linked characteristics

Certain characteristics of the canary are termed *sex-linked*. This is due to the fact that the particular gene involved is located upon the same chromosome as that which determines the sex of the individual. These chromosomes are designated X and Y and, in birds, the cock has two X chromosomes and the hen one each of X and Y so that, in breeding, the now familiar pattern is followed:

11 The mating of cock (XX) and hen (XY):

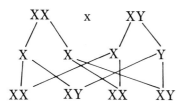

Results

50% cocks (XX) and 50% hens (XY).

Now, the genes for the melanin pigments are located upon the X chromosome and so they, and most of their mutations, are automatically linked with the determination of sex itself as mentioned in the entry on the *CINNAMON*. There, the various matings between Greens and Cinnamons were given, together with their expectations. Cinnamon colouring is recessive to the normal Green and so it is apparent that a cock bird can be of three different genotypes: pure breeding Green (GG); pure breeding Cinnamon (cc); and heterozygous Green (Gc) (i.e., visually green but a Cinnamon carrier). Hens, on the other hand, since their genetical

make-up contains only one X chromosome, can only be pure Green, or pure Cinnamon. There are no others.

Here only two of the possible matings concerning Greens and Cinnamons are given by way of illustration. (The symbols G for Green and c for Cinnamon have been used in the interests of simplicity although, in fact, the pigments involved are eumelanin (black) and phaeomelanin (brown).)

12 The mating of Green cock (GG) to Cinnamon hen (c'Y'):

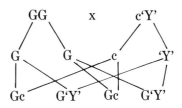

Results

All Green progeny, the hens being normal but the cocks being Cinnamon carriers.

13 Green cock, carrying Cinnamon (Gc) mated to Cinnamon hen (c'Y'):

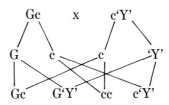

Results

25% Green cocks, carrying Cinnamon (Gc), 25% Green hens (GY), 25% Cinnamon cocks (cc) and 25% Cinnamon hens (c'Y').

Note

In this section on GENETICS, in the interests of clarity, symbols

Norwich

Right: Cinnamon Norwich, a colourful variety not widely bred

Far right: Heavily variegated White Norwich

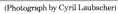

(Photograph by Cyril Laubscher)

Norwich Canaries of early days. These are quite different from their modern descendents (Cassell's "Book of Canaries and Cage-Birds")

A Norwich Canary in 1911 already showing development from the earlier type

Player's Cigarettes

Norwich Canary

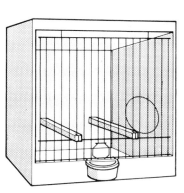

Show cage for Norwich Canaries

Badge of the Southern Norwich Plainhead Canary Club of Great Britain

have often been used that might offend the purist. For those who wish to go more deeply into the subject there are many books on genetics in general and on livestock breeding in particular. In many of these may be found not only a detailed explanation of various genetic problems, but also practical suggestions for maintaining and improving show points.

GERMAN CREST

This breed, among those recognized by the *Confederation Ornithologique Mondiale*, is virtually a Coloured Canary with a crest. Its breeding follows the usual pattern of that for any other crested breed i.e. Crest x Plainhead. It is most usually seen as a Red Canary with a dark crest.

Official standard

The standard of the *C.O.M.* is very brief and reads as follows:
CREST — Oval in shape, the central point clearly visible
PLUMAGE — Sleek
FORM — Shaped like colour canaries
COLOUR — As for colour canaries
CARRIAGE — As for colour canaries
SIZE 14cm
The scale of points allocated is as follows:

	Points
CREST	20
SHAPE	15
COLOUR	20
PLUMAGE	15
SIZE	10
CARRIAGE	10
GENERAL CONDITION	10
Total	100

GIBBER ITALICUS

(see colour feature page 127)

In the section on Frilled Canaries an outline was given of where this mutation first appeared and how it spread to other parts of Europe, where developments took place that resulted in the establishment of new breeds. The Gibber Italicus is one of these: a creation of Italian fanciers who have produced a bird which, to some eyes, possesses certain characteristics that are almost unnatural.

Its exact origin has not been recorded but, judging by visual appearance, it would seem almost certainly to be a derivative of the South Dutch Frill, probably with no other blood being involved. In general type and posture the two have much in common although the Gibber is a size smaller, being quite a slim and lightly-built bird and with less well developed frilling.

This tiny size has probably been brought about by the continued use of double yellow matings, which is the normal practice in this breed, instead of the traditional Yellow x Buff. Also, as a result of this procedure, a proportion of homozygous yellows are produced and these, in particular, have thin, scanty and sometimes brittle plumage which is a distinctive feature in the Gibber Italicus, although an objectionable quality in most other breeds.

Close inbreeding, which is commonly used in establishing a type, has also helped to produce a bird in which the naturally nervous action found in the frilled breeds has become exaggerated to an almost alarming degree, so that Gibbers often appear to be quite unsteady on their perches.

The Gibber is one of those breeds in which posture and frilled plumage have been combined. In show position it stands erect upon very stiff legs and with the neck thrust forward to give a posture in the form of a figure seven. The three main frills on shoulders, breast and flanks, are the only ones that should be present and, because of the scanty plumage, they are relatively rudimentary. The breast frills do not meet in the centre, thus leaving the breastbone exposed, and the feathering on the thighs is so sparse that most of this joint also is naked.

Official standard

The standard for judging the Gibber Italicus issued by the *C.O.M.* is as follows:
HEAD — Small, slender, serpent-like

BREAST — Frills symmetrical curving inwards, naked sternum
FLANKS — Frills curving outwards, symmetrical
THIGHS — Naked
UNDERPARTS — Smooth feathered
LEGS — Long and stiff, thighs exposed
NECK — Elongated, slender
MANTLE — Curving, symmetrical to left and right from centre of back
WINGS — Straight and close to body
TAIL — In straight line with back
SIZE — 14-15cm
POSITION — Forming a figure seven, neck extended and square with back

The allocation of points is as follows:

	Points
POSITION AND SHAPE	20
HEAD	6
NECK	15
LEGS	15
WINGS	6
SHOULDERS AND MANTLE	10
TAIL	6
JABOT — STERNUM	10
FLANKS	6
SIZE	6
Total	100

GIBBOSO ESPAGNOLE

This breed is very similar to the Gibber Italicus. However, it has an even more exaggerated posture with its head held well down below the horizontal in a similar manner to the old-time Belgian canary. It is alleged that this extra reach and length of neck has been achieved as a result of a mutation which has given the bird an extra cervical vertebra.

At the time of writing, no further details are available concerning the standards being pursued nor of any allocation of points for the various features.

GLOSTER FANCY

(see colour feature pages 26-27)

Many breeds of canary have origins that go back in time so far that little, or no, historic records were ever made of them. In the case of the Gloster Fancy, however, the matter is different since it is a relatively recent addition to the canary fancy. In fact, this most popular of all the crested breeds, first made its appearance upon the show bench in 1925, at the Crystal Palace, in London, although in a rudimentary form and not under its present title which was given to it later.

These original birds were bred by a lady fancier from Cheltenham, in Gloucestershire, England, and were said to have been produced by crossing crested Roller Canaries with the early 'wee gem' type of Borders. Later she was joined by other interested fanciers who also made use of small sized Crested Canaries crossed with the smallest of Borders available. Working towards an agreed ideal that was suggested by a leading judge of the day, by using this basic material and periodically exchanging stock, there gradually emerged the forerunners of today's small, neat, lively and prolific canary that has achieved such remarkable success in little more than half a century of existence.

After a somewhat slow start (they were not at first acceptable to the established elements in the canary fancy) the rise in popularity of the Gloster has been well-marked and consistent so that today it is the most widely kept of all the crested breeds. Because of the very freedom and ease with which they reproduce, the Gloster is one of those varieties that will commend themselves to the beginner. However, the highest standards of perfection are just as difficult to achieve as in any other breed of canary.

As has been explained elsewhere (see *CREST, CRESTED CANARY* and *GENETICS*), in all crested varieties there are two types that make up the breed. In the Gloster Fancy the crested birds are known as *Coronas* and the plainheads as *Consorts*. Following the normal breeding procedure, these should be mated together to produce on average 50% of each type among their progeny.

The official standard for the breed is issued by the Gloster

Red Canary

Red Canary associations flourish worldwide as can be seen by the badge of the Red Factor Canary Club of Australia

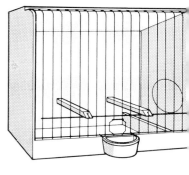

Show cage used for exhibiting Red Canaries in Great Britain

Intensive Red, still sometimes known by the earlier titles of Red Orange or Non-Frosted Red

Variegated Non Intensive Red (Apricot or Frosted Red)

Hooded Siskin from which the red coloration of the Red Canary has been derived

Convention, an organization embracing the twenty or so specialist societies functioning.

Standard of excellence

	Points
CORONA — Neatness, regular unbroken round shape, eye discernible	15
With definite centre	5
BODY — Back well filled and wings laying close thereto; Full neck. Chest nicely rounded without prominence	20
TAIL — Closely folded, well carried	5
PLUMAGE — Close, firm, giving a clear appearance of good quality and natural colour	15
CARRIAGE — Alert, quick, lively movement	10
LEGS and FEET — Medium length, no blemish	5
SIZE — Tendency to the diminutive	15
CONDITION — Health and cleanliness	10
Total	100

Standard of excellence

	Points
CONSORT — Head broad, rounde at every point with good rise over centre of skull	15
EYEBROW — Heavy showing brow	5
BODY — Back well filled and wings laying close thereto; Full neck, chest nicely rounded without prominence	20
TAIL — Closely folded and well carried	5
PLUMAGE — Close, firm, giving a clear cut appearance of good quality and natural colour	15
CARRIAGE — Alert, quick, lively movement	10
LEGS and FEET — Medium length, no blemish	5
SIZE — Tendency to the diminutive	15
CONDITION — Health and cleanliness	10
Total	100

Regarding the size, it will be seen that no actual figure is given, although in practice about 12.1cm (4¾in) is usually regarded as being the upper limit for a good show specimen.

GOLD

This term has two different meanings within the canary fancy according to whether it is used in connection with the Lizard or with Coloured Canaries.

1 In the Lizard, it is the Yellow bird of the breed as opposed to the Buff, which is termed *SILVER* (which see). The Lizard fancy has retained the ancient terminology for these two feather types which has served it throughout its long history of some two hundred years.

2 In Coloured Canary circles Gold is the term that has now been adopted for yellow-ground birds generally (e.g., Gold Agate, Gold Brown, Gold Isabel). These may be of either Buff or Yellow feather type in which case the distinguishing terms will be *NON-INTENSIVE* or *INTENSIVE* (which see) as the case may be.

GREEN CANARIES

In most breeds of canary, within the general colour range, green birds are to be found which, if they are completely free from any light feathering, are technically called *Self* Greens (see *CLASSIFICATION* and *SELF*). If there is any admixture of light feathers in the wings or tail, it places them in the category of *Foul* Greens. The green represents the wild-type of plumage pattern found in the canary before it became broken up with light feathering (Variegation) before finally leading to completely clear birds. For this reason, perhaps, many fanciers tend to disparage the Greens, or rather avoid having too many of them, since there is a tendency for the stock to revert to being predominantly Heavily Variegated or Green.

Greens do have their devotees, however, as do Cinnamons, and a really good Green can be a most attractive bird. The aim should always be towards having as pure and bright a green as possible, with the minimum of any tinge of bronze. For this reason Greens should never be colour-fed for exhibition (with one or two minor exceptions) otherwise the desirable grass green shade would be completely altered. The black pencilling on the back and flanks should be clear and distinct and not too broad and heavily laid. The beak, legs and feet should be as dark as possible (almost black), although light colouring in these parts is not actually a disqualification.

It must always be appreciated, however, that in all of the type breeds it is the correct bodily conformation that comes first — colour being a secondary consideration — so that many of the Greens seen on the show bench are not necessarily good examples of their colour. The best are nearly always to be found among the Borders, Fifes and Yorkshires. Among the Coloured Canaries, the Gold Greens, as one might expect, are of quite a brilliant green whereas, in the red series, they are a deep bronze-red.

GREENFOOD

Even the non-fancier is well aware of the value of greenfood in the canary's diet, as witness the household songster with groundsel or lettuce pushed between the wires of his cage. The nutritional value of greens is not high as they contain about 90% water, but they do provide a welcome change from the continuous hard seed diet. More importantly, they supply some of the much-needed vitamins and minerals if these are not given as additives in the water or soft food.

Most of the greenstuff grown in the garden for human use can also be offered to canaries. This includes such items as lettuce, spinach, cabbage, broccoli, kale and turnip tops. These and other produce from the greengrocer's shop, such as watercress, mustard and cress, chicory, endive, Chinese leaves, etc., provide another source of supply for town dwellers.

Many of the common weeds from the garden or countryside are also appreciated by the birds among which, at various seasons of the year, may be mentioned dandelion, groundsel, chickweed, shepherd's purse, sowthistle and many others.

Some fanciers are so keen on providing greenstuff for their birds that they offer it all the time. There is probably no harm in this provided that the birds' systems are accustomed to it. Most breeders offer it rather more sparingly, say twice a week throughout the winter months, increasing it to every other day as spring approaches, and finally daily in the week or so prior to pairing the birds up.

GRIT

Canaries need to be supplied with grit which they swallow to help grind up their seed. This grit, which is retained in the gizzard, eventually becomes worn down so that fresh supplies must always be readily available. Fanciers who have access to supplies of sea sand or sharp sand, can make use of these substances but, unless the source is known to be unpolluted, it would always be wise to wash and drain the sand well before offering it to the birds.

Most fanciers, however, purchase supplies of grit from their petfood suppliers. This provides a very wide range of the birds' digestive requirements by containing a variety of different grits such as flint, sand and limestone, plus granulated charcoal and often mineral additives as well. To avoid wastage, it is better not to use these relatively expensive grits as a floor covering for the cages, as might be done in the case of ordinary sand. Offer the supplies in small containers that can be topped up, or completely renewed, weekly at cleaning time. The common plastic two-hook drinkers are useful for this purpose or, cheaper still, small shallow potted meat or paste jars.

GRIZZLED

Instead of the normal dark markings on the head, body, wings or tail, some canaries occasionally have much lighter, greyish ones

Fife Fancy Canary
with a grizzled
marking on its neck

the crested breeds, where grizzled crests are quite common and separate classes are normally to be expected. In the case of the Lancashire Canary, which is ideally only a clear bird, a Grizzled Coppy is the only departure that is permitted. In dark-plumaged birds like Lizard Canaries, any grizzled feathers in wings or tail, or indeed anywhere else on the body, where the feathers should be as near to black as possible, are considered a very grave fault.

GROUND COLOUR

This can be defined as the natural basic colour of the bird's feather after the removal of all the dark (melanin) pigments. Technically it is known as the *lipochrome* colour. Originally the only ground colour in the canary was yellow, hence the emergence of the familiar clear yellow canary more than a couple of centuries ago, following the final disappearance of all markings. New ground colours have appeared, either by deliberate breeding as in the case of the Orange (or Red Orange) Canary or by mutation as in the cases of the White, Ivory and Rose. The two latter are from the same mutation but producing different visual effects upon the yellow, and on the red-orange ground colours. In the case of the white ground colour, there have been two different mutations giving rise to the Dominant and Recessive White (see relevant entries, also *GENETICS*).

which are termed *grizzled*. If these grizzled feathers are examined, they will be found to be either of a plain, even grey, or a mixture of minute black and white, or grey and white speckles, thus giving a dark or light grizzle as the case may be. Such markings are of no great significance and a grizzle-marked bird should normally be entered in the same class as a corresponding dark-marked bird, unless of course there are separate classes provided.

This is usually the case among

GROUND COLOURS

COLOUR	HOW PRODUCED
Yellow	Natural ground colour of the canary
Orange	Yellow + Red introduced from Hooded Siskin (*Spinus cucullatus*)
White	Yellow either suppressed, or lacking
Ivory	Dilution of yellow lipochrome to a pastel shade of ivory
Rose	Dilution of Red Orange to a pastel shade of rose

H

HAND-FEEDING

If the parents fail to feed their chicks in a satisfactory manner, it may be necessary to resort to hand-rearing, which some fanciers undertake with considerable success. Nevertheless, it is a very demanding exercise, both in terms of patience and the time involved, and is perhaps only to be recommended for the saving of really valuable stock. It is always a difficult decision to make, especially for the beginner, in resolving whether to start hand-feeding, or to leave well alone. If in doubt, the advice of an experienced fancier in the local bird club can be sought.

Some hens fail to feed their offspring from the outset and the chicks will then die after the first 24 hours; others will make a tentative start but the chicks begin dying at around the three-day mark. Still others will feed perfectly well for about ten days, and everything seems to be going splendidly when, for some reason or another, they seem to lose interest and stop feeding their growing brood.

There is always the natural anxiety on the part of the breeder to see whether his hens, especially any untried ones, will feed, but it is advisable not to disturb any newly-hatched nest in order to find out. If the hen does not readily leave the nest to collect food (and many will not do so as long as there is anyone in the room) the best plan is to finish off the routine tasks in the usual manner and then quietly depart, but leave the door of the birdroom open slightly so that observation can be made.

At the ten-day-old period it is quite easy to detect whether the youngsters are not being fed. At this stage they are normally stretching up vigorously for food so that one can see whether their crops are frequently empty, although at a later phase they will have become weakened and may possibly not reach up to be fed. They may however continue to gape in a half-hearted manner. At this stage, too, they are regularly excreting over the edge of the nest so that the absence of any fresh droppings will be a sure indication that no food has recently been given.

If hand-feeding is to be undertaken it must be appreciated that the chicks will need quite frequent feeds, at intervals of at least every two hours, throughout the day and up to late evening, hence the emphasis on how demanding this task can be. A syringe of some type will be needed — one in which the plunger can be completely withdrawn so that the food can be placed inside and the egg food mixture (see entry under *EGG FOOD*) will need to be of a fine and soft enough consistency to enable it to pass through the nozzle without clogging it. As an alternative, a small spatula can be used, or the end of a matchstick when the chicks are quite tiny, although it takes much longer to complete a feed in this way.

A little practice will be required before becoming adept at this operation and it will soon be discovered that it is not enough merely to put the food into the chicks' beaks, but well down their throats, otherwise they are unable to swallow it. An odd thing about non-feeding hens is that they will generally continue to brood their chicks so that the problem of having to keep them warm does not often arise. Once they are beginning to fledge nicely, however, it is better to take them right away and, in any case, the hen will by then probably be wanting to go to nest again.

Many theories have been put forward concerning the reasons why some hens do not feed, ranging from simple things like the food not being to their liking, to more complex ones like hereditary traits. The problem is what to do with such hens. In the case of unflighted birds, it is often recommended that they be given another chance, but once a hen has clearly proved herself to be an unreliable mother there is really nothing for it but to put her down. It is patently unfair to sell such a bird, or even to give her away for someone else to cope with. If she is of exceptionally high exhibition quality, of course, placing her eggs under a *FEEDER* can be resorted to as detailed under that heading.

HAND-WASHING

At one time the hand-washing of birds preparatory to entering them for a show was a recognized and unfailing routine among fanciers but nowadays it is doubtful whether it is practised to the same extent. Although the atmosphere of our towns and countryside may well be polluted with various noxious chemicals, at least it is not now laden with smoke and soot as it was in former days and so our birds are less liable to become dirty.

Indeed, if normal attention is given to the cleanliness of the birdroom and its cages, and the birds are allowed the regular use of the bath, it may be possible for them to go through the whole of the show season without any need for washing at all. Nevertheless, it is recogized that a bird that has been hand-washed and received careful preparation for a show can have an enormous advantage over its rivals and many experienced fanciers would never dream of shirking the task.

Like many other practical task, once the principles are mastered, it becomes a relatively simple undertaking without any particular hazards for the unwary. Naturally, however, the beginner attempts his first hand-washing with a certain amount of trepidation until growing confidence will enable him to carry on with it as easily as any of the other tasks in birdkeeping.

Most of the older handbooks on canaries advised that the novice

Materials for handwashing a canary

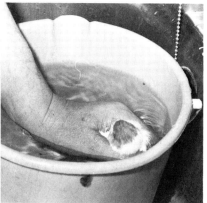

Immerse in warm water except for the head

Apply soap lather working in the direction of the feathers

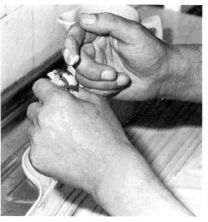

With the finger, gently clean head and neck

(Photographed by Cage and Aviary)

Rinse in cool water, removing all traces of lather

Dry the bird with a cloth to remove most of the excess water

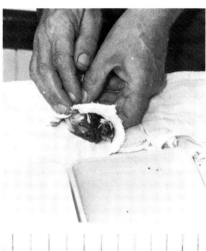

Roll up in a second cloth to allow further absorption of water

Place the bird on a clean towel inside a drying cage

(Photographed by Cage and Aviary)

should first attend a demonstration given by his local bird club; annual hand-washing demonstrations, prior to the show season, are organized by many of them. There is no doubt that this is as good a way to learn the procedure as any but, should the reader have no access to this facility, the accompanying series of illustrations may prove helpful.

HARTZ
From the eighteenth century onwards, the Hartz Mountains region of Germany became the centre of a thriving canary breeding home-industry which, at its peak, exported hundreds of thousands of birds annually to other parts of Europe and to the Americas. These were the specially raised and carefully trained songsters later to become generally known as Roller Canaries. So great was the reputation of these birds that, for a long period, Hartz Mountain Rollers became the advertising slogan of many an importer and bird dealer. In the United States the term *Domestic Hartz* is still in use for the section devoted to these birds at shows.

HATCHING
When hatching becomes due, thirteen or fourteen days after the hen was set, beginner and old hand alike are naturally very anxious to discover whether or not any young ones have materialized. Undue curiosity must be curbed and on no account should the sitting hen be flushed off the nest at this stage. Signs that hatching has, in fact, taken place will be the presence of empty egg shells on the floor of the cage and, if the fancier listens quietly, he will also hear the faint cheeping of the newly-hatched chicks.

If nothing has happened at the expected time, however, there is no cause for disappointment as it is not at all unusual for the eggs to be a day late in hatching. Fanciers have, from time to time, reported successful hatchings from up to three or four days late but this is exceptional. It can generally be reckoned that, if the eggs have failed to hatch after forty eight hours beyond the expected date, they are not going to do so. (For possible causes see *FERTILITY* and *DEAD-IN-SHELL*.)

There is no remedy at this stage, however, and the hen should be given about one week's break before being reconditioned and put to nest again. If the eggs were clear, a check should be made that any possible cause for infertility was not overlooked; for example, the trimming of long feathers from around the vent area.

HEAD

The shape of the head in any exhibition type of canary is of some fair importance and many are the variations that have been developed over the years. In fact, *A Study of Heads* was the subject of an illustration in one of the old standard works on canaries (*Our Canaries*, by Claude St.John, 1911). Nearly all of the breed Standards start by describing the

head and it is often the first feature that anyone, including the judge, tends to look at.

In the Border and Fife Fancies, for example, it should be small, neat and round, with the eye centrally placed. In the Norwich, it should be large and bold, with a full forehead above the beak, and well rounded both over and across the skull. In the Yorkshire, it should be full and round with the line of the back of the skull carried well down the neck to meet the shoulders. With such breeds as the Scotch Fancy and the Belgian, on the other hand, the head should be oval and sleek and, in the case of the Gibber Italicus, even to the point of being snake-like. The Crested breeds, of course, have their own particular adornment in the form of a topknot of specified shape and proportion, each according to its own ideals. The Lizard is unique in having a light coloured cap covering the crown of the head and following almost exactly the outline of the skull.

Whatever may be the fancier's

A selection of contrasting heads: Gloster Corona; Border Fancy; Belgian; Parisian Frill; Norwich Plainhead; and Scotch Fancy

own particular choice of breed, he should always concentrate upon ensuring that in his birds the head is correct, for failures on this point are, perhaps, one of the major reasons for lack of success on the show bench.

HEATING

It is often asked whether it is necessary to provide heating in the birdroom. In countries with a reasonably temperate climate the answer is 'No', but it should be added that, although not strictly necessary, it is often a matter of convenience. Any fancier will confirm this after experiencing a spell of wintry weather when the birds' drinking vessels freeze solid day after day.

If properly acclimatized, the birds themselves, however, have no real need of artificial heating for, unlike wild birds whose resources are severely tested during prolonged spells of bad weather, they are never short of food which provides the calories to maintain bodily heat and keep them in good condition. Therefore, if heaters are installed, it should be done with an eye to preventing the freezing up of water vessels and not with any idea of forcing the birds into early breeding condition by the use of unnaturally high temperatures.

In cool climates, many fanciers make use of electric tubular heaters, thermostatically controlled with the setting at about 5°C (40°F), the number and size of heaters depending upon the size of the birdroom. Advice on these matters could be obtained from the experience of fellow fanciers or from an electrical supplier. The use of any type of naked flame heaters, even with proper safeguards, should be viewed with suspicion. Accidents can happen and it would, indeed, be tragic to lose an entire stock in a fire.

HEAVILY VARIEGATED

Variegation, by definition, is the existence of areas of dark feathering upon the otherwise clear body of the bird. The only

Heavily Variegated Cinnamon Border Fancy Canary

question that needs clearing up is, 'Where is the dividing line between Lightly Variegated and Heavily Variegated?' The commonsense answer, of course, is at the 50/50, or halfway stage but few of the specialist societies actually say so. Among those that do are those of the Yorkshire canary which state in their classification:

'1. Lightly Variegated, more light than dark.

2. Heavily Variegated, more dark than light.'

For birds that are particularly heavily variegated, some clubs, notably those of the Border and Fife Fancies, include a special category of 'three-parts-dark' which, again by their definition, 'must be 75% dark'.

There are always some birds that will be borderline cases, and which sometimes get wrong classed, but any reasonable judge should accept a bird of this kind as entered unless it is quite clearly, in his opinion, well beyond the accepted limits of the definition.

HEMP SEED

This large, round, greyish seed is not available in some countries. It is a great favourite with canaries and they will generally pick it out first from any general mixture. Hemp has a very hard coat and the birds will often spend ages in turning it round and round in their beaks until they are able to make the first incision and start shelling the husk. Young, newly-weaned birds, in fact, are usually quite unable to do this and fanciers will often feed them hemp that has been lightly crushed. Even soaking it generally fails to soften the outer skin. In the past, hemp seed germinated and sprouted quite readily but, today, it does not do so. This is apparently because in many countries it is treated to prevent it from being used for growing marijuana, but whether this has affected its feeding value for canaries is open to question.

Hemp is a seed with a high oil content and is said to be rather stimulating and fattening if given in excess. It is probably wise, therefore, not to offer it in unlimited amounts, although many fanciers affirm that they use it quite freely during the breeding season without ill effects.

HERVIEUX

Many of the larger treatises on canaries make mention of this early authority. Hervieux was the first writer to give any detailed information about the bird as it existed in his time — the late seventeenth and early eighteenth centuries. In his book *Traité des Serins de Canarie*, first published in 1709, he gave an interesting list of the varieties known to him. These were not breeds in the sense that would be understood today, but merely the many forms of plumage variation that had occurred since the bird's domestication. Most of his descriptions are fairly easily identifiable as the different forms of marking and variegation that are still recognized by fanciers today, but some cannot be explained satisfactorily in the light of modern genetics.

Some of the older commentators sought to identify one or two of Hervieux' varieties with certain ancient breeds like the Lizard, London Fancy and Dutch Frill, but this was entirely a matter of

conjecture and cannot be accepted as fact. The only thing that can now be inferred is that, by Hervieux's time, the canary had reached a stage in its development when the plumage had broken up into pied or variegated patterns and that a clear yellow bird had already emerged, which he said was the most rare at that time.

HOODED SISKIN

The Black-hooded Red Siskin (*Spinus cucullatus*) is important in being the source of the red pigment that has now been added to the canary's genetic make-up and is clearly in evidence in the Red Canary. Mules and hybrids are generally known to be sterile but, over 70 years ago, it was discovered that the male hybrids between the Hooded Siskin and the canary (known at the time as *copper hybrids*) often proved to be fertile. By mating these again to canaries, eventually a strain of orange coloured birds was evolved which were the forerunners of the present Reds.

This work was not simple as, in the F_2 generation, there was a high degree of infertility among the cock birds; and the hens, in fact, were not found to be fertile until the F_4 generation, and so progress was inevitably slow. Pioneer work persisted, however, and has resulted in a whole new field of canary culture as exemplified by the Coloured Canaries in general and the Red Canary in particular.

HOPPERS

Most seed hoppers available today are of a universal design and made of transparent plastic material.

(see colour feature pages 62-63)

A selection of seed hoppers commonly used by canary fanciers

(Photographed by Cage and Aviary)

They are entirely suitable for their purpose, having smooth surfaces and rounded corners, and are very easy to clean. They provide a minimum of opportunity for any insect pests to find a hiding place.

Slightly less suitable, perhaps, are the so-called self-supplying seed hoppers which are used in aviaries and flights. Unlike their counterparts used by poultry keepers, they need frequent attention. Whereas poultry swallow their pellets whole, thus allowing fresh supplies to slide down into place, it is the habit of canaries to sit at the hopper shelling their seed. Because of this, the drawer eventually becomes full of seed husks and no new supplies can come down until these husks have been blown away.

HOSPITAL CAGE
Some fanciers regard a hospital cage as a necessity, others as a luxury, while many more probably do not possess one at all. Clearly, the aim of every fancier should be that of establishing and maintaining a healthy and vigorous stock of canaries and thus it might

A temporary hospital cage can be improvised in an emergency

On the other hand, especially in the case of valuable exhibition stock, it might be argued that it is worth the effort to treat any bird that is not suffering from any serious or contagious complaint. For this purpose, a hospital cage is the best answer. Such cages can be purchased, completely equipped, from the manufacturers but are rather expensive. However, if over the years they are responsible for saving the lives of many valuable birds, the initial cost will have proved negligible.

Hospital cages can quite easily be constructed by any fancier who is capable of basic cage-making skills. The main essentials for such a cage are that:

1 It should be of a convenient size for easy handling, say about the dimensions of a single compartment in a breeder (i.e. approximately 46 x 40 x 25cm (18 x 16 x 10in);

2 It should have a source of low heat capable of maintaining a temperature of about 27°C (80°F), for example, a 60-watt domestic light bulb or something similar.

3 It should have provision for a sheet of glass or clear plastic to fit over the front to exclude draughts.

When treating a sick bird, the floor of the cage should always be covered with white blotting paper, or some of a similar absorbent quality, so that observation can be kept on the state of the bowels. Drinking and feeding vessels should be of a kind that can easily be removed for washing and disinfection.

(Photographed by Cage and Aviary)

A specially designed hospital cage for the treatment of sick birds

be argued that the retention of any sick bird, that has not made a fairly rapid recovery, is not going to be an asset since inherent weaknesses may well be passed on to future generations.

73

I J

INBREEDING

The procedure known as inbreeding consists of the mating together of closely related individuals, such as father and daughter, mother and son, brother and sister, and so on. It is a technique now well understood and often widely used by geneticists and experienced breeders of livestock but needs to be handled with extreme caution by the uninitiated. The pioneer livestock improver of the eighteenth century, Robert Bakewell, for instance, is generally held to have been very successful in his work with one particular breed and yet to have ruined another.

Inbreeding results in the concentration of various hereditary characteristics, both good and bad, so that it is just as likely to produce inferior birds as good ones. The skilful breeder, of course, ruthlessly eliminates what he regards as rubbish and inbreeds again with the best specimens. Even these may still be carrying undesirable features that have yet to come to the surface and so the purifying process has to continue. For an appreciation of how recessive characteristics may be carried through several generations before coming to light, refer to *GENETICS*.

In theory, the end result of a prolonged programme of inbreeding would be a strain of birds so genetically stable that they would be virtually all alike. This state has been reached in the case of certain laboratory animals, such as rats and mice, which have to be genetically identical for the experiments that are carried out on them to be valid.

Probably very few canary fanciers ever indulge in a really serious and scientifically worked out programme of inbreeding and it is certainly not to be recommended to the beginner who has only a limited stock of birds. In any case it is a waste of time to inbreed with birds of only moderate quality for, at best, it will only result in perpetuating mediocrity.

INCUBATION

The period of incubation in the canary is thirteen or fourteen days. At the commencement of this period, when the hen will be set, it is advisable to clean out the cage, quietly and without fuss, before returning the real eggs to the nest so that there should be no further disturbance while she is sitting. A decision will have to be made as to whether to leave the cock bird with the hen, or to remove him altogether. Many fanciers do the latter and leave their hens to sit and to rear their youngsters entirely on their own, which the majority will usually do perfectly well.

Nevertheless, it cannot be denied that a good pair, working well together, will produce a thriving nest of rapidly growing chicks in the minimum of time so that, for a start, it may be advisable to leave the pair together and see how things develop. Some cock birds will pass the time sitting contentedly on the perch and singing their time away, but others are restless and mischievous, often interfering with their sitting partner or pulling the nest about. If this is the case, it is better to take the male away rather than risk having the eggs broken.

During the incubation period some breeders keep their sitting hens on a very plain diet, such as canary seed and water only, but many others prefer to leave the diet unaltered, except to offer small quantities of the greenfood, soft food, etc., as it becomes due. In this way the bodily metabolism is neither subjected to unnecessary change, nor does it become over stimulated.

INO

This is one of the newer mutations in the realms of colour breeding and, as such, is of specialized interest to the scientifically minded fancier. It appears to be a rather puzzling mutation and experimental breeders have reported that its visible effects can take various forms. Some are difficult to recognize and need a close study of the disposition and density of both melanin and lipochrome colours within the web of the feather. The most attractive of these forms is said to give a hammered copper pattern to the plumage, which is unknown in any other mutation.

In the Brown and Isabel series of birds (Red, Rose, Gold or Ivory) the underflue of the feather is beige of pale brown, while in Greens and Agates it is dark or pale grey respectively. One other unusual characteristic of the Ino is that the birds have a bright ruby red eye which, unlike the pink eye of Cinnamon canaries, does not change in adulthood. Like the variable plumage patterns, the intensity of the red eye colouring does vary within the mutation and it has been pointed out by some breeders that Inos tend to have weak eyesight, even a disposition towards blindness. With careful selection of suitable breeding material, however, this fault may eventually be eliminated.

The Ino mutation is found to be a homozygous recessive, and so matings and their expectations will follow the inheritance tables shown for similar mutations under *GENETICS*.

INTENSIVE

This is a European term that has been accepted in Coloured Canary circles elsewhere. It is the equivalent of the yellow bird in the type breeds and is applied to birds with this type of feather, whatever the colour series to which they belong. Thus there are the Intensive Red, Intensive Rose, Intensive Gold, and so on, although many fanciers still prefer to use the older alternative term of Non-frosted which clearly identifies this feather type as being the one without frosting.

ISABEL

The Agate Canary, already mentioned is, in effect, a dilute green because its melanin pigments are in a paler, or diluted, form. This mutation had its effect upon both eumelanin and phaeomelanin pigments so that, in the case of the Cinnamon Canary, a dilute cinnamon was the result. This was called the *Isabel* in continental Europe and the term has now been accepted in Coloured canary circles elsewhere. As with the Agate, it can be allied to any of the lipochrome ground colours to give Red Isabel, Rose Isabel, Gold Isabel, Silver Isabel, etc. Of these, the first mentioned (the Red Isabel) is regarded as a real classic

---

EXPECTATIONS FROM NORMAL AND IVORY MATINGS

	PARENTS	PROGENY
1	Ivory cock x Ivory hen	All Ivory
2	Normal cock x Ivory hen	Normal hens, normal cocks carrying Ivory
3	Ivory cock x normal hen	Normal cocks, carrying Ivory. Ivory hens
4	Normal cock carrying Ivory x normal hen	Normal cocks, normal cocks carrying Ivory, normal hens, Ivory hens
5	Normal cock carrying Ivory x Ivory hen	Normal cocks carrying Ivory, Ivory cocks, normal hens, Ivory hens

among Coloured canaries and is often considered to be one of the most beautiful in this section of the fancy.

IVORY

Birds of this mutation first appeared in Holland about 1950. They have the normal yellow ground colour diluted to an even shade of ivory throughout the plumage. The mutation has also been known as *lipochrome pastel* on account of its effect upon the lipochrome colours, i.e., turning yellow into the pastel shade of ivory, and red into the pastel shade of rose (see *ROSE*). The characteristic is recessive and sex-linked in the manner of its transmission and so follows a similar inheritance table to that of the Cinnamon. It is quite a straightforward matter to keep Ivories along with a stock of normal yellow ground Coloured Canaries.

JAPANESE HOSO

This breed has been developed by Japanese fanciers mainly from imported Scotch Fancy stock. It is a miniaturized form of the Scottish breed, a slim and lightly built bird.

Official Standard

It has been recognized by the *C.O.M.*, which has issued the following Standard and Scale of Points:

HEAD — Small and oval
BREAST — Narrow
BODY — Long and tapering
THIGHS — Just visible
LEGS — Slightly bent
NECK — Long and fine
SHOULDERS — Very narrow
WINGS — Closely carried
LINE OF BACK — Curved
TAIL — Long and narrow. Carried under perch
POSITION — Semi-circular
SIZE — 11 to 12cm
PLUMAGE — Smooth without frills

	Points
SHAPE	25
SIZE	10
HEAD and NECK	10
SHOULDERS and BODY	15
POSITION	30
TAIL	5
CONDITION	5
	Total 100

JONQUE

This term may be encountered in some of the very oldest manuals on canaries. It was specifically applied to that ancient breed, now extinct, the London Fancy. It was the term for what is now called *Yellow*. The word is now quite obsolete in the canary world but, strangely, does persist to some extent in the British Bird section of the cage bird fancy where it still may be used to describe birds of the yellow-feather type.

JUDGING

Although the ratio of judges to exhibitors may not be high, it is desirable that there should be a steady supply of new ones coming along to replace older ones as they retire from the arena. But it is not everyone, however earnest their intentions, who will necessarily make a competent judge.

The successful judge is not automatically the person who has committed to memory all of the written standards and scales of points but more likely the one who has a good eye for a bird and a clear mental picture of what the ideal should look like. Obviously, a successful career as a breeder and exhibitor should provide a sound

L

background for any judge, but there are many fanciers who keep one breed of canary only and are scarcely interested in any other. At the larger shows specialist judges are usually appointed but, at many of the smaller events, a judge may be required to handle more than one variety and so he will need to be familiar with breeds other than his own.

Some specialist societies have trainee judging schemes whereby an aspiring judge can serve an apprenticeship under one or more old hands until he has gained sufficient experience and he may then be appointed to the judging panel. In addition to this, some also have a written examination to ensure that the applicant does have the necessary factual knowledge.

A judge has a certain amount of clerical work to do. This will involve:

1 Checking that each class set before him is correct in number and tallying with the entries in his judging book;
2 If any exhibit should be absent, finding out if this is known to be correct, or if the bird has accidentally been overlooked and left on the benches. (An efficient show secretary will have ensured that there is no problem here by providing the judge with a list of known absentees.)
3 After judging each class, entering the results in his judging book and sending a duplicate slip to the show secretary;
4 Keeping a record of the specials winners after checking that they are eligible to compete for the said specials. (Again, the show secretary should have provided all of the necessary information on this point.)

Unlike some hobbies, a canary judge is not required to make written comments upon the merits, or otherwise, of each exhibit. It is customary for him to remain in the show hall for some time after the public has been admitted and to make himself available to discuss points with any exhibitor who may wish to do so.

LACING

This term is used in the Lizard Canary section of the fancy (see *LIZARD*). It refers to the edging on the feathers of the wing coverts, both the greater wing coverts, which protect the flight feathers, and the lesser wing coverts on the shoulders and wing butts. These feathers should be basically black and have a nice contrasting margin

Lizard Canary showing lacing on the wing coverts

of colour so that they appear to be well and distinctly laced, with no suggestion of clouding or haziness blurring the edges.

LANCASHIRE

This famous old British regional breed is of special interest. It actually became extinct but has lately been revived. This has been achieved by fanciers making use of two breeds which, in the past, had received a lot of Lancashire blood in their own making: the Crested Canary and the Yorkshire. By crossing selected specimens of

(see colour feature pages 30-31)

these and retaining the most suitable offspring for further work, birds have now emerged which measure up fairly well to the Lancashire of former times.

The old-time Lancashire was established as far back as the 1820s or 30s and was developed throughout the Victorian era until it reached its peak towards the end of the nineteenth century. Its popularity, however, never extended far beyond its own native county although it was extensively used by breeders of the Crested and Yorkshire canaries in the improvement of their own varieties. Due to these demands, and not being notably prolific, the numbers of Lancashires fell. Between the two World Wars it was in the hands of very few fanciers and it is doubtful whether more than a mere handful of birds survived into the post-war period. Fortunately, the efforts to revive the breed have been successful, although it is still in far too few hands for safety.

Like the Crested Canary and the Gloster Fancy, it is found in the two forms which are known here as *Coppies* (crested birds) and *Plainheads*. One essential difference between the Lancashire and other breeds, however, is that in the Lancashire all the birds should have clear plumage with no markings or variegation of any kind being tolerated. The sole exception to this is that the crest itself, in the coppy bird, may be grey or grizzled without incurring any penalty.

In the course of breeding, Lancashires occasionally crop up which have faint grizzled marks on the body or wings. Such birds, although not suitable for show, can be used for breeding provided that their antecedents are known and the fault is not likely to be perpetuated. A further interesting point is that the Lancashire holds the distinction (shared only by the Parisian Frill) of being the largest breed in the canary world — 20cm (8in) long, and sturdily built to go with it — so that every endeavour should be made in selecting

breeding stock not to allow size to deteriorate.

The Official Standard for the Lancashire Canary consists of a written description, followed by a scale of points:

'The Lancashire should be a large bird, of good length and stoutness, and when in the show cage should have a bold look. The Coppy should be of a horseshoe shape, commencing behind the eye line and lay close behind the skull, forming a frontal three-quarters of a circle without any break in its shape or formation, and should radiate from its centre with a slight droop. There should be no roughness at the back of the skull. The neck should be long and thick, and the feathers lying soft and close, the shoulders broad, the back long and full, and the chest bold and wide. The wings of the Lancashire should be long, giving to the bird what is called a long-sided appearance. The tail should also be long. When placed in a show cage the bird should stand erect, easy and graceful, being bold in its appearance, and not timid or crouching. It should not be dull or slothful looking, and should move about with ease and elegance. Its legs should be long and in strength match the appearance of the body. When standing upright in the cage the tail should droop slightly, giving the bird the appearance of having a slight curve from the beak to the end of the tail. A Lancashire should neither stand across the perch nor show a hollow back. It should have plenty of feather lying closely to the body and the feather should be fine and soft. The properties of the Plainhead are the same as the Coppy, with the exception of the head. The head should be broad and rather long, the eyebrows clearly defined and overhanging or what is called lashed. The feather on the head should be soft and plentiful, and not look tucked or whipped up from behind the eye into the neck. The aim in breeding should be to keep and improve the size and length of the bird, at the same time losing nothing of its gracefulness, its beauty of feather and general contour.'

Scale of points

HEAD — Coppy	30
NECK — For fullness and thickness	10

Back — Round, full and long   10
Length of Bird and Substance
                             25
Upstanding Position and Type 15
Condition and Cleanliness   10
                   Total 100

LAYING

The subject of egg-laying has been largely covered in other entries in this book (see *CLUTCH, DUMMY EGGS, EGGS, EGG-BINDING*). They are summarized here.

1 Egg laying may be expected to commence within about a week or ten days after pairing the birds up, although variations of some days either way can occur according to season and the condition of the breeding pair;

2 Signs of the impending event are: the hen roosting in, or near, the nest at night, and an increase in the consumption of water for some 48 hours beforehand.

3 Eggs are laid singly and at 24-hour intervals, normally in the early hours of the morning.

4 Breeders remove the eggs as laid and substitute them with dummies until the fourth egg has appeared when they are returned to the nest for the hen to incubate.

5 The average number of eggs in a clutch is four, and breeders work on this assumption, but five is quite commonplace and even larger clutches can sometimes occur.

6 The only problems that are likely to present themselves at this period are:
   a hens that occasionally lay their eggs on the floor of the cage (a thick covering of sawdust will prevent breakage);
   b hens suffering from egg-binding (see notes on this subject);
   c eggs sometimes being broken by an over-inquisitive cock bird.

LEGS

Under the subject of *HEADS* it was pointed out how this feature varies from breed to breed, and it is much the same in the case of the birds' legs. Clearly, a tremendous degree of variation is not possible and such differences as there are occur mainly in length, shape and set of the leg. Even these may not be noticed by the casual observer unless they are pointed out to him.

Canaries notable for length of leg are mainly those breeds with an upstanding posture, usually combining length of body as well. These include the Yorkshire, Lancashire and Scotch Fancy among British breeds, and the Belgian, Parisian Frill and other frilled varieties among other European ones. Relatively short legs are to be found in the Norwich and Crested Canaries, while the remainder have legs of medium length. These include such breeds as the Border, Fife, Gloster, Lizard and Coloured Canaries.

The set, or position of the legs relative to the body, will clearly have a considerable effect upon the bird's stance; legs set well back will tend to produce a bird that stands across the perch at a fairly low angle, e.g., the Norwich and Crested Canaries. Legs set higher up will assist in the correct posture of the upright school of birds mentioned above, whereas the many breeds of intermediate size with a position ranging between 45 and 60 degrees from the horizontal, have legs set in what might be termed a more normal position. All of this may not be immediately apparent to the uninitiated until a closer study is made of some of the leading specimens on the show bench.

Finally, regarding the shape of the legs, the only differences to be seen here are connected with the flexibility of what could be called the knee or elbow joint (neither term is anatomically correct, but will serve). In most breeds this will be of normal suppleness, producing ths usual flexible bend in the joint, but remarkably, in several European breeds, notably the Belgian and Gibber Italicus, this joint is very stiff thus giving rise to the typical stilty legs of those varieties which are almost straight from thigh to foot. This feature is apparently connected in some way with the unusual figure 7 posture of these particular breeds.

LICE

All birds are known to be susceptible to infestation by various kinds of parasites, many of them peculiar to their own particular host species. In hygienic conditions, canaries can usually remain relatively untroubled by these pests and it should be the aim of every fancier to be proud of the fact that his stock of birds is free from parasites. However, even in the best run establishments, they may be introduced occasionally and unwittingly from outside agencies, so it is as well to be prepared for them.

The most common lice to affect canaries are small, greyish insects about 2.5mm (one tenth of an inch) long, which are permanent parasites, spending their whole life cycle upon the body and only leaving it in order to infest another bird. They are feeders upon skin and feather tissue and thus can cause a good deal of irritation which can clearly be seen by the fact that the birds are continually scratching and pecking at their plumage — not, however, to be confused with normal preening.

If any bird is suspected of harbouring lice, it should be caught up and examined in the hand, gently blowing the feathers apart. If the pests are present, they will be seen running about among the underflue of the feathers. Various methods of treatment can be applied, which involve using either an insecticidal powder or a liquid spray, both of which are available from the usual fanciers' suppliers. The manufacturer's directions should be carefully followed. These generally involve repeat applications to deal with any subsequent hatchings of the pest which is not destroyed in the egg stage of its life cycle.

Whichever method is used, it is important to get the material well down into the underflue and close to the skin where the lice live; it is useless merely to treat the web of the feather. The closest attention is usually needed in the neck, abdomen and rump areas where the bird finds itself less able to dislodge the pests and, after treatment, any bird should first be placed in a spare cage with paper on the floor and left there for half an hour, after which it may be returned to a clean stock cage and the paper burnt.

LIGHTING

As in the case of heating, artificial lighting in the birdroom is not a necessity and most breeders will do without it if they can. However, the circumstances of a fancier's job may compel him or her to attend to the birds either early in the morning, or in the evening after returning from work which, in the winter time, might be in the hours of darkness. If it does become necessary, it is essential to fit the lighting system with a dimming device so that the birds are not obliged to flutter around in the dark after the lights have been switched off in an effort to regain their perches, when of course injury might occur.

There are some fanciers who, contrary to the general practice, go in for early breeding (often quite successfully) and who freely use artificial heating and lighting to enable them to do so. A beginner is not advised to adopt this system — at least until he or she had gained some basic experience in breeding.

LIGHTLY VARIEGATED

This is the category in which a bird having less than half of its plumage of a dark colour is placed (see also *HEAVILY VARIEGATED*). It is very rare, however, for the two to be given separate classes at any show: Variegated, Yellow or Buff, Cock or Hen, Flighted or Unflighted, as the case may be, being the usual form of classification.

LINE-BREEDING

Many fanciers will state that they use a system of line-breeding with their stock, but it is not at all clear whether they are all using similar methods since the term may have different implications. It may be:

1 A modified form of inbreeding involving the mating of less closely related individuals such as cousins, or uncle to niece, nephew to aunt, and so on;

2 Establishing a direct line of descent from a particularly outstanding individual by mating him first to his own daughters and then to the resulting grand-daughters, etc., so that there is an ever increasing percentage of the original blood (i.e. genes) in the stock;

3 Running several separate and distinct family lines within the stud so that whenever an outcross is needed it can be achieved with known material from one of the other lines and no necessity to introduce a bird of unknown performance from elsewhere.

All of these methods are used by some of the leading exponents of the art of canary breeding and have much to recommend them given the correct circumstances. However, as in the case of *INBREEDING* (which see), it is useless to embark upon this form of exercise with only moderate foundation material.

Many books on the general

Lightly Variegated
White Border
Fancy Canary

aspects of livestock breeding will outline a plan for developing a line-bred stud of birds or other animals but it must be realized that this is mainly theory and must be applied with commonsense according to the excellence, or otherwise, of the material being used and in the light of the results being achieved. A rigid plan that has brought success to one fancier in no way guarantees a similarly favourable outcome for another.

LINSEED

This flat, brown seed comes from the flax plant and is usually included in small amounts in any general seed mixture for canaries. It has a very high oil content and is alleged to improve the sheen on the bird's plumage if given during the moult. An old-fashioned practice, which is still used by some fanciers, was to boil some linseed, producing a sticky jelly-like substance. This is incorporated in the soft food before feeding it to the birds. If linseed is present in any seed mixture intended for soaking, this ability to exude a sticky jelly can be a nuisance.

LIZARD

The Lizard is the oldest breed now in existence and was clearly described in a manual for fanciers as long ago as 1762. Here the author referred to the birds as 'The fine Spangled Sort ... which a few years ago was brought hither from France but since much improved in colour and beauty by English breeders.'

This statement probably accounts for the origin of the tradition that the Lizard owed its introduction into Britain to the Huguenot refugees from France. It would appear, however, that the breed eventually died out in continental Europe since none were to be found there until fairly recent times following importations from Britain during the past thirty years or so.

Apart from its antiquity, the Lizard is unique in another respect: it is now the only variety of canary left to us that is bred

(see colour feature pages 50-51)

Scotch Fancy

Scotch Fancies of the nineteenth century showing the curved posture that is once more in vogue

This show cage has remained unaltered during the course of the breed's history

Present day Scot Fancies. Breed are aiming to create the earl standa

Player's
Cigarettes

Scots Fancy
Canary

Early twentieth
century Scotch
Fancies showing
the exaggerated
posture produced
by cross breeding
with Belgian
Canaries

entirely for the pattern of markings on its plumage. Experimental work suggests that this was brought about as the result of a mutation in the normal wild type of feather pattern. The most important of these markings are the *spangling* on the back, the *rowing* on the breast and the *cap* on the crown of the head, this last feature being the only one where actual clear feathers are to be found, the remainder of the body being dark as in a Self Green Canary.

Fanciers also attach great importance to the depth and richness of the ground colour in their birds. In this breed the two basic feather types are known as Gold (i.e., Yellow) and Silver (Buff). The effect of colour feeding is to produce a deep chestnut ground colour in the Golds and a warm shade of bronze grey in the Silvers. The black markings superimposed upon this background, together with the black wings and tail and the orange coloured cap, produce a most striking bird which is entirely different from any other breed of canary.

In view of the fact that all birds of this breed are dark-plumaged Selfs, apart from their caps, the classification is based upon the variations that are found in this feature which are detailed in the official standard which follows. Since it has never been easy to produce top class exhibition specimens, plus the fact that, owing to the unusual nature of the mutation, the Lizard is in its perfect show plumage for one season only, this breed has never enjoyed widespread popularity. During the Second World War, in the hands of very few fanciers, it only just survived. Happily, it is now in a flourishing state once again with, possibly, more admirers than at any time in its long history.

The official standard for the breed, issued by the Lizard Canary Association, consists of a full written description and a scale of points:

'It should be noted that Golds and Silvers, Capped or Non-capped, Cocks or Hens, may all attain an equal standard; and that broken-capped birds which are equal to the ideal in all respects other than the cap, will lose only a proportion of the ten points for the cap (or the ten points for perfection of the spangling on the head of the non-capped birds) according to the extent of the blemish in either case.'

In the interests of brevity and convenience, one model has been chosen for description. It is a Gold Cock, clear capped.

'The bird is 4¾in (12.1cm) in length (see Note 1), neither over-stout nor too slim. It stands quietly and confidently on the perch at an angle of 45 degrees. The ground colour is uniform in depth and is a rich golden bronze (Note 2) entirely free from any suggestion of other shade (Note 3). The spangling is clear and distinct, each individual spangle being clear of another. It extends from the edge of the cap in perfectly straight lines to the wing coverts, each succeeding spangle being proportionately larger than the one nearer the neck.

The feather quality is of conspicuous silkiness (Note 4), the feathers being close and tight with no suggestion of coarseness or looseness.

The breast is round and fairly full without giving any appearance of stoutness. The rowings are clear and distinct from one another and are lineable. They extend along the bird from near the eye down to the base of the tail and across the breast from both sides well towards the centre.

The wing feathers are compact and held closely to the body. Their tips meet in a straight line down the centre of the back. They are so dark (except on the extreme edges) as to appear black (Note 5).

The tail is narrow, straight and neat with feathers of the quality and colour of the wing feathers (Note 6).

The head is fairly large, round and full on the top. The cap extends from the beak to the base of the skull and is oval in shape with a clearly defined edge. It is clear of the eye, being separated therefrom by the eyelash which is a well-defined line of dark feathers extending to the base of the upper mandible (Note 7). There are no dark feathers between the cap and the upper mandible. The cap is of a deep golden-orange colour and has no blemish of dark or light feather.

The covert feathers are clear, distinct and lineable and so dark as to appear black. They are distinctly laced around the edges.

The beak, legs and feet are dark.

The bird is in perfect condition, quite steady and staged correctly.'

Scale of points

SPANGLES — For regularity and distinctness	25
FEATHER QUALITY — For tightness and silkiness	15
GROUND COLOUR — For depth and evenness	10
BREAST — For extent and regularity or rowing	10
WINGS AND TAIL — For neatness and darkness	10
CAP — For neatness and shape	10
COVERT FEATHERS — For darkness and lacing	5
EYELASH — For regularity and clarity	5
BEAK, LEGS AND FEET — For darkness	5
STEADINESS AND STAGING	5
Total	100

Condition is taken for granted. A bird which, in the opinion of the judge, is not in perfect health or which shows any physical defect, shall not be credited with any points for other virtues.

In classes for non-capped or nearly non-capped Lizards, points are awarded to a maximum of ten for the perfection of spangling on the head.

Notes

1 It should not exceed 5in (12.7cm) in length. It is considered an equal fault to be either undersized or oversized.
2 It is customary to colour-feed Lizards. This has the effect of giving them a warmer tint, turning the golds to a rich chestnut colour and the silvers to a warm silver-grey.
3 Any tinge of green or suggestion of smokiness is a serious fault.
4 In silvers, it may be described as velvetiness. The silver Lizard should possess a deep ground

colour of a warm buff tone. Over mealiness is to be discouraged.
5 The blacker the better.
6 In overyear birds the presence of a tiny fleck of white on the tail or wing feathers is not considered to be any detriment.
7 Should the light feathers extend too far down the back of the neck the bird is said to be *overcapped*. This is considered a serious fault. Should they extend down past the eye or beak the bird is said to be *bald-faced*. This fault renders the bird unfit for exhibition.

Definitions

THE CLEAR CAP — A Clear Cap Lizard is one whose cap is perfectly clear of dark feather or feathers and has reasonably regular edges.

THE NEARLY CLEAR CAP — A Nearly Clear Cap Lizard is one whose cap contains a dark feather or feathers covering an area not exceeding one-tenth of the total area of the cap.

THE NON-CAP — A Non-capped Lizard is one whose head and neck are quite clear of light feathers.

THE NEARLY NON-CAP — The Nearly Non-cap Lizard is one whose head and neck are marked by light feather or feathers to an extent not exceeding one-tenth of the normal area of a Lizard's cap.

THE BROKEN CAP — A Broken-capped Lizard is one whose head and neck feathers disqualify it from being classed either as a Clear or Nearly Clear-capped, or as a Non- or Nearly Non-capped.

LONDON FANCY

Little need be said about this breed which effectively became extinct during the First World War, although continuing in a degenerate, crossbred state with one or two fanciers into the 1930s. It was a breed of equally ancient date to the Lizard. Similarly, it was bred for its plumage pattern which, in its perfect form, was quite striking, consisting of a clear golden-yellow body with contrasting black wings and tail. From time to time a new generation of fanciers conceives the idea of recreating the breed but

Yorkshire

A Variegated
Yellow Yorkshire
Canary
photographed in an
aviary. In a show
cage the bird would
adopt a more
upright posture

The long slim
Yorkshire Canary
as it was in the
1930s

Yorkshire Canaries
from the
nineteenth
century. This early
type is quite
different from the
modern bird

The badge of one of
several Yorkshire
Canary clubs that
cater for this breed

Show cage for the
Yorkshire Canary,
specially designed
to emphasize the
Yorkshire's
upright posture

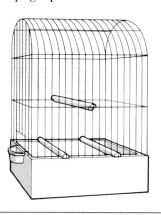

Yorkshire Canaries
as they had
developed by the
early twentieth
century

Nineteenth century engraving of a London Fancy Canary before the breed became extinct

this is quite an impossible task since the mutation which gave rise to it has now been lost.

LONGEVITY

Newcomers to the fancy usually wish to know how long a canary may live. When kept purely as a household pet, they have not infrequently been recorded as having lived for 10, 12 or even 15 years when kept in ideal conditions. Exhibition stock may only average five to six years, possibly due to the demands and stresses of the breeding room and the show bench. However, like human beings, some may not attain their alloted span while others may well live beyond it.

LUMPS (FEATHER TUMOURS)

This disfiguring condition occasionally affects canaries, more commonly in some breeds than in others, causing disappointment to their owners since they are then no longer fit for exhibition. These lumps may vary in size from that of a hemp seed to something as large as a hazelnut. They occur mainly on the wing butts, shoulders and back. The tumour consists of impacted feather tissue which, if cut open in an early stage of development, also contains a lot of blood. Later, when the tumour has dried up it may be removed

without too much distress to the bird.

Little is definitely known about the cause of these lumps. At one time they were alleged to be due to the practice of double-buffing (pairing together two Buff birds) and yet some breeds which have been double buffed for generations (e.g., Parisian Frills or Scotch Fancies) never seem to suffer from the condition. There may be some affinity with the crested gene since all crested breeds suffer from lumps from time to time, and yet certain other non-crested breeds can also occasionally be affected.

It is also often said that the problem is an hereditary one and the only way of avoiding it is to refuse to breed with any affected bird. However, although this is obviously a sensible course to follow, it is not the simple answer to the problem because a bird may well be three or four years old before ever developing a lump and will therefore have already been bred with and, in any case, careful records through several generations have failed to establish any hereditary connection.

Although this affliction is regarded with some apprehension by fanciers, it is, in fact, not at all widespread and even in strains knows to be affected by lumps, these may not appear in more than 5% of individuals.

M

MANAGEMENT

This term might broadly be interpreted as covering the whole spectrum of canary culture, even including such specialized activities as breeding, moulting, preparing for exhibition, and so on, which are fully dealt with elsewhere in this book. Here, however, the more general aspects of the subject are intended and it will soon become apparent that a system of efficient management is likely to make the hobby more enjoyable. Too many fanciers, perhaps, go through relatively long spells of giving their birds the minimum of attention which is then necessarily followed by a flurry of activity in carrying out those tasks that ought to have been spread over a longer period.

From the very outset, therefore, even with a relatively small stock of birds, it is advisable to organize one's routine into jobs that require doing daily, weekly, and occasionally, at longer intervals.

Daily tasks are fairly easily attended to, consisting merely of feeding and watering the birds. Seed hoppers will need to have the loose husks blown from them and then topped up with seed. Any additional items of food can be supplied by reference to a feeding chart which is useful to have pinned up somewhere in the birdroom (see earlier entry under the heading *DIET*). Water pots should be emptied, wiped clean and then refilled with fresh water. This, in particular, should never be neglected as stale, dirty water can obviously be detrimental to the birds' health. Certain types of floor covering, such as newspaper or sand, may also need to be changed daily although the majority of fanciers use sawdust which, being much more absorbent, needs to be renewed less often.

Weekly tasks are mainly those connected with cleaning out the birds' cages. In most cases this will involve the following routine:
1 *BATHS* (see earlier reference);
2 Wiping the cages clean and dry;
3 Changing to clean sawdust on the floor;
4 Washing and replacing perches;
5 Fresh supply of grit in the grit pots;
6 Sifting the seed from the seed hoppers and replenishing the supply;
7 Washing the water pots and any feeding receptacles that have been used.

When performing these various tasks, the value of the double-breeder type of cage will become apparent, as it is a simple matter to run the occupants of the cage into one half, using the wooden sliding partition, while cleaning out the other side. If only single cages are being used if will usually be necessary to run each bird out into a show cage.

Occasional tasks will mostly be those of a seasonal nature such as spring cleaning the birdroom preparatory to the breeding season, minor repairs and repainting as they become necessary, cleaning and disinfection of any cage that has had sick birds in it, cleaning out show cages after their return from a show, and so on.

Meticulous fanciers may make a list of the various management tasks as outlined above and pin it up in the birdroom, ticking off the items as they are done. Such is the nature of the perfectionist, but perhaps most fall well short of this ideal!

MARKINGS

Allusion has already been made to the various markings to be found in the canary when dealing with the subject of classification and details of the technicalities of even-markings were given under that heading. Similarly, the definitions of *LIGHTLY VARIEGATED, HEAVILY VARIEGATED, THREE-PARTS DARK*, and *FOUL* have been given.

American Singer

Developed in the United States, this breed sets out to combine the song of the Roller with the type of the Border Fancy

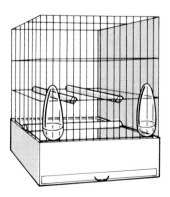

A distinctive feature of the American Singer show cage is the solid side wall which is there to prevent the birds seeing each other during singing contests

Columbus Fancy

As with all crested breeds, this exists in plainhead and crested forms. American fanciers have produced this bird by the blending of several English breeds

Show cage for the Columbus Fancy Canary

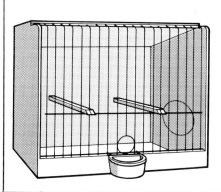

The Columbus Fancy has long been a popular breed in the United States, as this American Cage-Birds Magazine from the fifties shows

DEFINITIONS OF MARKINGS

CLEAR	No dark feathering present. Usually any dark underflue is disregarded, provided it does not show on the surface. Any dark marks on legs, feet or beak are also disregarded.
TICKED	Any *single* dark mark which may be: **a** on the body — coverable by a 1p piece **b** in the wing — not more than 3 adjacent feathers. **c** in the tail — ditto.
LIGHTLY VARIEGATED	More light feathers than dark.
HEAVILY VARIEGATED	More dark feathers than light.
3-PARTS DARK	75% or more of the feathers dark.
FOUL*	A dark plumaged bird possessing: **a** on the body — a single area of light feathers coverable by a 1p piece; **b** or in the wing — not more than 3 adjacent light feathers. **c** or in the tail — ditto. *Some authorities will accept any number of light feathers in the wing or tail, provided that there are none on the body.
SELF	Dark pigmentation throughout. No light feathers anywhere on body, wings or tail.
TECHNICAL MARKS	1 Evenly marked birds which may be: **a** six-pointed — marked on each eye, secondary flight feathers and outer tail feathers; **b** four-pointed — any even combination of four technical marks; **c** two-pointed — any even combination of two technical marks. 2 Unevenly marked birds which may be: **a** five-pointed — possessing any five of the technical marks; **b** three-pointed — possessing any three technical marks.

By way of recapitulation it may be recalled that the original wild canary, when first domesticated, was of the self-green type with no light feathering at all. In course of time, as happens with most species of birds and animals under the influence of domestication, the markings break up into pied, or variegated, patterns. Many of these were described as long ago as 1709 by the French writer Hervieux. These broken patterns continued progressively until they culminated in the appearance of the completely yellow bird.

The aims of breeders in Britain and in Europe generally, since early in the nineteenth century, have mainly been in the direction of type rather than markings so that most of the present-day breeds of canary continue to exhibit the whole range of plumage variations from self to clear.

MATING

This term is sometimes used by fanciers in its narrower sense to denote the actual act of copulation, but more often in the general aspect of pairing the birds up at the beginning of the breeding season. This is commonly accomplished by placing the two partners in their breeding cage but separated by a wire slide for a day or two so that they can get to know each other. If wire slides are not available the same result can be achieved by using a wooden sliding partition. It should not be pushed quite to the back of the cage, but a gap left of about 1.3cm (½in) which allows the pair sufficient contact at this stage.

During this period the cock bird will, if fit, spend a lot of time singing at the hen and eventually feeding her, which is a common courtship activity in the canary and serves to create the pair bond. When they can be seen to be getting on well, the slide can be withdrawn and the birds allowed free access to each other. Usually all will go quite amicably but occasionally a particularly ardent cock bird will chase the hen around. This is nothing to be alarmed at, unless it becomes clear that the hen is distressed by his attentions, in which case she is not really quite breeding fit. Sometimes the reverse is the case and a dominant hen will bully the cock, but unless serious bickering takes place, there is usually no need to separate them again.

Many pairs are quite placid and undemonstrative and the fancier may never observe copulation. The ultimate appearance of a nestful of healthy chicks will verify that it has occurred.

MAW SEED
This is the very tiny bluish-grey seed of a commercially grown poppy. It has a high oil content and is usually included in condition seed mixtures, and small amounts are often added to egg food preparations. For birds that may be a little off colour some bread and milk sprinkled with maw seed often has a beneficial effect.

MEALY
This was an early fanciers' term for what we now call Buff. It was particularly applied to the now extinct London Fancy Canary. Fanciers still occasionally use the word, especially when referring to the amount of frosting on a Buff by saying that it is too mealy, or of a Yellow possessing the fault of being mealy on the back, etc.

MELANINS
The dark pigments found in the canary's plumage are called *melanins*. They consist of a black pigment (*eumelanin*) and a brown one (*phaeomelanin*) and, if both are present on a normal yellow-ground bird, the familiar self-green colouration is the result. (According to some authorities there are two forms of the brown pigment but this is probably only of interest to the more scientifically minded fancier). If the black pigment is lacking the well-known mutant form the Cinnamon is produced (see *CINNAMON*). For those who keep white-ground birds the two equivalent colours are Blue (both melanins present) and Fawn (brown melanin only).

A whole series of mutations have taken place affecting the melanin pigments in one way or another, some of which have been mentioned elsewhere. They mainly concern the dilution, or density, of the melanins and their disposition over different areas of the feather, thus giving rise to the many interesting plumage patterns such as the Opal, Pastel, Ino and Satinette.

MENDEL
It was the Austrian monk Gregor Mendel (1822-1884) who first made a scientific investigation into the inheritance of certain well-defined characteristics in living things and their numerical relationship, and so laid the foundation of the modern science of genetics. When applied to canaries this has enabled us to understand the relationship between Yellow and Buff, Green and Cinnamon, Crest and Plainhead, etc, and to predict the outcome of various matings of this nature. Test matings following Mendelian principles are an

Fife Fancy

(Photograph by Cyril Laubscher)

Fife Fancy Canaries: Clear White and Clear Yellow. This miniature breed, developed from the Border Fancy, has become increasingly popular during the past few decades

(Photograph by Cyril Laubscher)

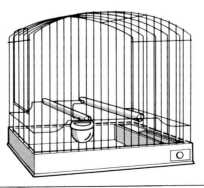

The show cage for the Fife Fancy is the same as that for the Border Fancy with the exception of having narrower perches

Wild Canary

A pair of wild canaries, still found in some Atlantic islands

The original wild canary from which the modern breeds are derived (Our Canaries)

essential prelude to establishing any new mutation that occurs. (See also *GENETICS*.)

MILAN FRILL

Many years ago some of the fanciers in the city of Milan were specializing in the breeding of a pure white frilled canary, known then by the name of *Milano Bianco*. In size and type, and in the formation of its frills, it was practically identical to the Parisian Frill. More recently, two other colour forms have been admitted to the breed, Clear Red Orange and Self Blue. No other colour is permitted at present. The birds must always be of one colour only with no broken patterns, such as the markings and variegation common to most other breeds, being allowed.

Official Standard

The standard drawn up for the Milan Frill by the *C.O.M.*, who also give it the alternative name of Colour Frill, is as follows:

NECK — Well frilled
MANTLE — Formed by abundant feathers which are divided by a central longitudinal parting between the wings to fall as symmetrically as possible over the shoulders
BOUQUET — Continuation of the mantle
COCK FEATHERS — Falling abundantly on each side of the tail

TAIL — Long and robust
HEAD — Abundant frills
WHISKERS
COLLAR — (Neck)
BIB — (throat)
JABOT — Well furnished, forming a shell
FLANKS (Fins) — Starting from the femur on each side of the bird to rise concentrically around the wings
VENT AND THIGHS — Frilled
NAILS — Formed like a corkscrew
SIZE — 18cm
CARRIAGE — Elegant and proud
COLOUR — One colour: white, red-orange and blue
PLUMAGE — Soft and voluminous

	Points
COLOUR UNIFORM	15
SIZE (18cm)	10
PLUMAGE	15
CARRIAGE	10
JABOT	10
FLANKS	15
HEAD	5
WINGS	5
TAIL	5
MANTLE	5
GENERAL CONDITION	5
	Total 100

MINERALS

A number of mineral salts are known to be essential for the proper functioning of the body processes, many of them in such minute quantities that they are known as *trace* elements. Most of these one would normally expect to be present in the diets that are usually provided for canaries in the form of various seeds, greenstuffs, seeding weeds, soft foods, and so on. Many fanciers, however, guard against any possibility of mineral deficiency by using *mineral supplements*, either purchased separately or ready mixed with the birds' supply of grit or soft food. They are generally listed on the label of the container by name or by their chemical symbols, i.e., calcium (Ca), phosphorus (P), magnesium (Mg), potassium (K), iron (Fe), iodine (I), sodium (Na), chlorine (Cl), manganese (Mn) and sulphur (S). If the fancier is intending to mix the supplement with his own foods, he should always keep strictly to the instructions of the manufacturer; no extra benefit can be obtained by giving stronger doses.

MOULTING

The moulting season is another of the major phases in the canary fancier's year and a very important one, especially for the keen exhibitor. Coming immediately after the breeding season, it sees all of the adult stock undergoing a complete change of plumage and the youngsters of the year moulting their body feathers (but not their wings and tails) to become the 'unflighted' birds for the autumn shows. The season starts about the middle of summer and continues until the middle of autumn, or thereabouts. Individual birds do not take all this time to complete their moult, the process usually occupying about six to eight weeks.

The first sign that a bird has commenced to moult will be the appearance of a few stray feathers in the cage or on the birdroom floor. New feathers first appear on the pectoral tracts and on the wing butts and the fresh bright colour shows up well against the old faded plumage. The casting of feathers then proceeds in an orderly fashion, gradually extending over the whole body and finishing up on the head and neck. It has often been stressed by experienced fanciers that the moult can make or mar a bird for the coming show season and so careful attention to detail at this stage is obviously of utmost importance.

Once they have started to moult, the birds are best not disturbed unduly. It is wise to place them in good time in the cages it is intended they should occupy. Any sudden change of environment may cause a bird to stick in the moult which might prove troublesome to restart. This could result in patchy colouring, especially with varieties being colour-fed.

Frequent bathing assists in the casting off of the old feathers and the emergence of new ones from their quills. Many fanciers will provide baths daily during this period, or alternatively spray the birds lightly with tepid water.

Varieties that are being colour fed will need to be started on this preparation before any feathers start to fall otherwise the new plumage may emerge paler in shade than may be desired. Similarly, as the moult nears its close, the colour food will need gradually to be decreased to ensure even colouring throughout the plumage.

Promising birds that are likely to form part of the fancier's show team are best caged singly in order to minimize any possible damage to their new plumage. This is particularly important in the case of Lizard Canaries.

During the moulting period birds are somewhat susceptable to extremes of temperature. If necessary, it is therefore sensible to close the birdroom windows each night and be prepared to switch on the heating.

Feeding during the moult should be on the generous side with items that are high in protein which is essential for the formation of feather tissue. At the same time, since the birds are rather less active than usual, care must be taken to avoid fattening foods. Most fanciers provide a standard seed mixture in the seed hoppers, plenty of greenstuff and seeding weeds, a little egg food two or three times a week, and condition seed occasionally, increasing its quantity towards the end of the moult, to enhance the sheen or *bloom* on the plumage.

MULES

An interesting sideline for many canary breeders lies in the production of *mules* — which is the bird fancier's term for hybrids of which one parent (usually the female) is a canary. Over the years many examples of these canary mules have been bred, all of them interesting and many of them very colourful indeed so that they form a small, but important, section at cage bird shows.

(see colour feature pages 54-55)

In Europe generally, and Britain in particular, most of the mules are produced by crossing the males of various members of the finch family with canary hens so that we have the Goldfinch Mule, Linnet Mule, Greenfinch Mule, Siskin Mule, Redpoll Mule and so on. The male Bullfinch, on the other hand, is not a ready hybridizer and so, in this instance, the cross is made the other way round by using a male canary and a female Bullfinch. Examples of all of these crosses are usually to be seen on the show benches at most European shows.

Aviculturists have also produced a great many other hybrids with the canary, mostly by using other members of the same genus (*Serinus*) but as most of them differ little in appearance from the wild canary they have never been taken up by the fancy.

Most mules are sterile and so further breeding with them is rarely attempted. One important exception to this was the cross between the South American Black-hooded Red Siskin (*Spinus cucullatus*) and the canary. Fertile hybrids from this alliance laid the foundations for the present breed of Red Canaries which now form an important section of our shows.

If mule breeding is seriously considered the aim should always be for the production of exhibition specimens since ordinary mules are of little value. For exhibition purposes the fancier recognizes two categories: the dark mule and the light mule. The former is a dark plumaged bird as in a Self Green Canary and the latter (which is quite scarce and extremely difficult to produce) should be Clear, Ticked or lightly marked. Anything in between, with ordinary variegated plumage, is of no consequence to the fancier and would never be considered on the show bench.

Of all the mules that are produced by breeders each season nineteen out of twenty are of the dark variety and these are perhaps the best kind for the beginner to attempt. Size, quality and colour are all important features of the dark mule which should, of course, also show clear evidence of its parentage. A good Dark Yellow Mule of, say, the Goldfinch, Greenfinch or Bullfinch can be of a superb colour and most attractive in appearance and for the breeding of these the canary hen that is required would be a Yellow Self Green, preferably of the Norwich type. Buff Green hens will only produce Buff mules which, nevertheless, can be quite excellent birds but without the richness of colour of the Yellows.

It might be imagined that Light Mules could be produced by using Clear canary hens instead of Selfs but such is not usually the case. Most of the progeny turn out to be Three-Parts Dark or nearly so. The Light Mule is, in fact, an elusive creature and many fanciers have tried for years without producing one — and yet it might unexpectedly turn up quite by chance! Years ago breeders put their faith in what they called *sib-bred* canary hens — that is, hens that had been produced by close inbreeding for many generations using only clear birds with no dark blood in their ancestry, but even these gave no more than the occasional Light Mule.

Some fanciers maintain that the finch holds the key to the secret but, here again, dozens of them may have to be tried out before one might be found that would sire the occasional Light Mule. One certain thing is that a genuine Light Mule (preferably a Clear) is extremely valuable and exceptional prices have been paid for a specimen of this description.

Finches for use in mule breeding may be obtained from British bird fanciers who, since the advent of conservation legislation, have been breeding them in aviaries instead of obtaining birds from the wild. These finches should be housed in aviaries or large flights throughout the winter months along with the canary hens that they are intended to partner. If any show a preference for each other's company they may be caged up together and their partnership

Munchener Canary

encouraged in readiness for the breeding season. It is the natural order of things for birds to pair up only with their own kind and so the mule breeder has difficulties to overcome in encouraging what are, after all, unnatural relationships.

Breeding procedure follows somewhat similar lines to that of canaries with a few added difficulties such as the fact that some finches, particularly the Goldfinch, are normally very late in coming into breeding condition. The timing of pairing therefore needs careful judgment. It is usual to shut off the finch each evening by means of sliding partition when the eggs are due to be laid. Few of them are to be trusted with eggs when confined in a cage — although they are less likely to be destructive when flying in an aviary. Similarly, if kept in a cage, it is better to allow the hen canary to do all the rearing of the youngsters as the male finch may not be entirely trustworthy.

Young mules grow very rapidly and may leave the nest earlier than young canaries. They are also inclined to be rather wild and it will need patience to steady them down. When weaned they need much the same follow-up treatment as young canaries. Most mules should be colour-fed during the moult if they are intended for exhibition.

MUNCHENER
This breed of canary from the city of Munich has a minor following elsewhere in Europe and has never been seen in Britain. It has something of the style of the Scotch Fancy but without the exaggerated curvature of that breed.

Official Standard
It is on the list of varieties recognized by the *C.O.M.* with the following standard:
HEAD — Very small
BREAST — Narrow and rounded
LEGS — Long and slightly bent
NECK — Long and narrow
SHOULDERS — As narrow as possible

WINGS — Long and tightly braced
TAIL — Long and narrow
PLUMAGE — Smooth
SIZE — 15-16cm
SPECIFIC ATTITUDE — Line of the head, neck and back slightly curved

	Points
POSITION	20
HEAD AND NECK	20
BREAST/SHOULDERS/WINGS	20
TAIL	10
LEGS	10
PLUMAGE AND COLOUR	10
IMPRESSION	10
Total	100

MUTATION
This term refers to various changes in the appearance of the canary which have represented departures from the normal. Examples have been the crest and the frill (feather formation) and the Cinnamon and the Agate (colour). A mutation occurs as a spontaneous change in the constitution of one or more genes in the bird's hereditary make-up and, if this results in a quite startling new visible form as in the examples quoted above, it is eagerly seized upon by breeders for further development. Some interesting mutations have unfortunately been lost to us as, for example, the famous old London Fancy canary.

NEST FEATHER

This has already been mentioned in earlier references dealing with the bird's age and with moulting. It is the first coat of feathers developed by the nestlings which will last them until their first moult begins at the age of ten to twelve weeks. Then, with the exception of the flight feathers of the wings and of the tail, the whole of the body feathers are renewed and will last for the ensuing year.

In Britain, many of the local cage bird societies hold a Nest Feather show in July for the special purpose of exhibiting these young birds. However, some fanciers believe that they are far too immature to undergo such a strain on their bodily resources — though others say that the experience does them no harm. Either view may be correct according to the state of development of the youngsters concerned but it is certainly inadvisable to exhibit any bird that is not yet weaned from soft food and not able to eat hard seed. (See also *AGE*.)

NESTING MATERIAL

Some canary hens are extremely slovenly nest builders, often making little attempt at it or, if they do, producing a very sub-standard job. On this account, and to provide an adequate anchorage for the nest of those that do build efficiently, it is necessary to have a nest pan lining, either stuck or sewn into the nesting pan. These linings are made of felt and can be purchased from the usual fanciers' suppliers, or they can be cut from a piece of carpeting underfelt, or some similar material. Sterilizing before use would be a sensible precaution.

Nesting material itself can also be purchased from pet shops or fanciers' suppliers, either in bulk or in small packets, but many fanciers prefer to provide their own. Keen gardeners who go over their lawns in spring with a wire rake will have ample supplies of dead grass and moss as a basis for nest making. First it should be given a thorough wash in a bucket of water to get rid of any dirt, and then boiled in order to sterilize it and kill off any insect pests that it may contain.

Like other finches, the canary hen likes to finish off her nest by lining it with finer, softer material such as cow hair. This can easily be collected on a country walk from barbed-wire, hedges, and so on, where cattle are kept. Again, sterilization is an important aspect. The material should be cut up into relatively short lengths so that it does not get entangled in the birds' claws. As an alternative, the carpeting underfelt already referred to, can be teased out into a suitably fine texture for the final lining.

Small wire nesting material racks which hang onto the cage fronts are useful for supplying the material to the breeding pairs, or it can merely be tied into small bundles and hung up inside the cage. Either way, the birds usually pull it all out and scatter it around a good deal before getting down to the serious business of nest building.

NIGER SEED

This is a small black seed, some 5mm (⅕in) in length. It is another seed of high oil content which is generally included both in basic canary mixtures and in condition seed. Many breeders are convinced that niger is an excellent preventative of egg-binding and thus give their breeding hens a pinch of the seed three or four times a week from mid-winter onwards.

NON-CAPPED

Lizard Canaries, apart from their caps, are all dark plumaged birds and so do not lend themselves to the classification that is used for

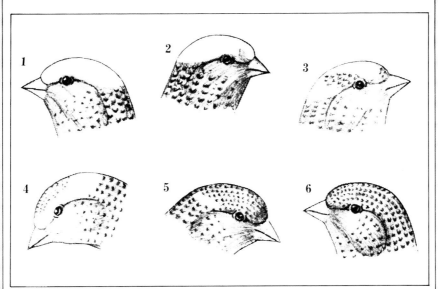

Heads of Lizard Canaries
1 Clear Cap;
2 Nearly Clear Cap;
3 Broken Cap;
4 Broken Cap (Patch Cap);
5 Nearly Non-Cap;
6 Non Cap.

other breeds. Instead this is based upon the variations that are found in the cap itself. (See *LIZARD*.) In the category known as Non-capped, the usual cap is completely lacking and is replaced by feathering of the normal spangled pattern of the breed. In a good specimen these tiny spangles can be really beautiful and Non-capped birds are firm favourites with Lizard devotees, not only on their own account, but as show specimens and for their value in the breeding room..

NON-FROSTED

This is the yellow type of feather found in canaries and is alternatively known as Intensive in Europe and in Coloured Canary circles in Britain. Ideally, they should exhibit no frosting whatsoever in their plumage although some birds do tend to suffer from this defect which is always considered a fault in exhibition specimens.

(see colour feature page 123)

NORTH DUTCH FRILL

Under the general heading of *FRILLED CANARIES* it was explained how a mutation in the feather formation appeared in Holland around the end of the eighteenth, or early nineteenth, century. This change in the normal type of smooth feathering gave rise first to the Dutch Frill and then to the many other frilled breeds of

canary that were developed from it in later years. In its country of origin, there still remains what might possibly be regarded as the prototype and now is known as the North Dutch Frill to distinguish it from others. It will be appreciated, however, that in almost two centuries of selective breeding, much improvement will have taken place so that the breed of today is in a more cultured state than its progenitors.

In the North Dutch Frill, the three basic frills mentioned in the earlier reference have been developed to perfection and no additional frilling is permitted. The mantle, craw and fins must be well-developed and completely symmetrical so that the balance of the frills, to left and right of the body, is perfect. Each frill should be voluminous but well-groomed in appearance without any misplaced feathering or roughness to spoil the effect. The head and neck at the one end, and the rump and abdomen at the other, should be normally feathered and quite smooth, as should the feathering on the thighs.

This breed is one of moderate size, being about 17 to 18cm (6¾in) in length, not so large as the Parisian or Milan Frills, but considerably more substantial than the tiny Gibber Italicus. It stands fairly upright on the perch at an angle of 85 degrees and with a slight bend in its posture. All of the usual range of colours found in other breeds of canary are also permitted in the North Dutch Frill.

Official Standard
The standard as laid down by the *C.O.M.* is as follows:
NECK — Clearly visible, fine, smooth
MANTLE — The feathers of the mantle are divided by a median and longitudinal parting to fall symmetrically over the shoulders
WINGS — Rather long, lying close to body
TAIL — Long, narrow
HEAD — Smooth
BEAK — Fine
BREAST — In the form of a voluminous heart
FLANK — Long, symmetrical, well raised up
UNDER BODY — Smooth
LEGS — Long, slightly bent, thighs covered with small, smooth feathers
ATTITUDE — Bold, 85 degrees
SIZE — 17cm

	Points
POSITION ERECT	15
SIZE (17cm)	15
FEATHERS OF MANTLE	15
FLANKS	15
FRILLS OF BREAST	15
ABDOMEN	5
HEAD AND NECK	10
TAIL	5
GENERAL CONDITION	5
Total	100

(see colour feature pages 58-59)

NORWICH

This is probably the most famous of all British breeds of canary and many fanciers know of the association of the British city of Norwich with canaries. This dates back well into the last century when canaries were being bred on a large scale in the city. Many thousands of birds were sent annually to the pet shops and street markets of London at a time when the canary was the favourite household pet among large sections of the population.

As an exhibition form, too, the Norwich was a prime favourite among fanciers in Victorian times and held this position for almost three-quarters of a century until losing some of its popularity to rapidly developing breeds such as the Yorkshire and Border. Even to this day, it is still probably in third place numerically among the fanciers in Britain and is to be found in many other countries throughout the world.

The Norwich breed is said to owe its origins to the Flemish refugees from the Low Countries. They brought the birds to Britain at a time when fancying in its various forms was on the increase. Oral tradition, of course, is not always reliable in detail but often the basic truths are firmly founded and so there is no reason to doubt the origin as it has been handed down to posterity.

Two great events, which had repercussions throughout the whole canary fancy, took place during the past history of the Norwich. The first of these was the introduction of the practice of colour-feeding canaries to enhance their colour for exhibition purposes (see *COLOUR FEEDING*) and the second was the dramatic change of type that occurred from the late 1880s onwards which was brought about as a result of outcrossing with another breed. Both of these events opened the eyes of fanciers to the possibilities of further development within their own breeds. Eventually no variety, except the Lizard, became entirely free from the effects of crossbreeding.

It was explained elsewhere how the breeders of the Crested Norwich first sought to improve their birds by the introduction of Lancashire Coppy blood into their stocks. This brought about quite dramatic results, not only in the development of the crest, but also in the size and length of their birds. Eventually, these ideas filtered through to the breeders of the Norwich Plainhead who either made use of the new type of crest-bred canaries, or actually crossed with the Lancashire Plainhead at first hand. A craze for sheer size

The Standard with Points

Feature	Description	Points
TYPE	Short and cobby. Back broad and well filled in, showing a slight rise transversely. Chest broad and deep, giving an expansive curved front, and sweeping under therefrom in one curve to the tail. Ideal length 6 to 6¼in. Stance or position at an angle of about 45 degrees	25
HEAD	Short and thick, continuing the run from the back skull on to the shoulder, and from a full throat into the breast	10
WINGS	Short and well braced, meeting nicely at tips to rest lightly, yet closely on the rump	10
TAIL	Short, close packed, and well filled in at the root. Rigidly carried, giving an all-of-one-piece appearance with the body	5
LEGS AND FEET	Well set back. Feet perfect	5
CONDITION	In full bloom of perfect health. Bold bouncing in movement	10
QUALITY OF FEATHER	Close and fine in texture, presenting the smooth, silky plumage necessary to give a clean-cut contour	10
COLOUR	Rich, bright and level throughout, with sheen and brilliancy. Yellows a deep orange. Buffs rich in ground colour and well mealed	10
STAGING	Clean and correctly staged in Standard Club Cage	5
	Total	100

quickly followed in which all other features seem to be lost sight of but, in due course, sanity returned and a reaction set in against these undesirable trends.

The Norwich had changed, however, and in 1890 new standards were introduced in which type, quality and colour were reinstated as the major features of the breed and the size was restricted to 16cm (6½in). Canary writers in the past have often referred to the Norwich as the John Bull of the canary world in describing its short, stocky, thickset figure. This, in essence is what it should be — allied also to close and firm feather quality, with a colour as rich and deep an orange as can be obtained.

The official standards of the Norwich Plainhead Clubs in Great Britain are given above.

NOVICE

Conditions governing the exhibiting of canaries may vary from country to country but, in Britain, any newcomer to the fancy is entitled to start his career in the *novice* category before graduating to champion status. The wording of the novice rule can differ slightly according to the club concerned but a fairly widely accepted rule defining a novice is as follows:

'A novice exhibitor is one who, at the commencement of the show season, has not won three first prizes in novice classes in open competition. Any wins in classes with less than three exhibitors and seven staged exhibits shall not count, neither shall wins in selling classes nor at events that are not fully open. An exhibitor commencing the season as a novice may continue to show throughout the season in that category irrespective of the number of wins gained.'

Some clubs set a limit on the number of years for which a fancier may remain a novice, after which he will be required to move up to the senior status but many novices choose to do this voluntarily after serving, say, five or six years apprenticeship in the hobby. To prevent any unfair practice, there is usually an addition to the novice rule stating that if two or more exhibitors are residing at the same address, they shall adopt the status of the higher one of them, e.g., it would not be possible for a father to show as a champion and his son as a novice, nor for a husband to be a champion and his wife a novice, and so on. For this reason, it is not uncommon for relatives to show in partnership.

OATS

This grain, although not of major importance, is sometimes fed to canaries. Red Canary fanciers in particular use it occasionally as a substitute for canary seed during the moult as it contains less lutein, and therefore aids in the intensification of the red in their birds' plumage. Other breeders sometimes use it in small amounts during the winter months and it can also be included as a constituent of a soaked seed mixture in the breeding season. It is generally obtainable from seed merchants in the form of hulled oats (groats), clipped oats or pinhead oatmeal.

OPAL

One of the many mutations in the Coloured Canary section of the fancy, the Opal, first occurred in Germany in 1949. Its effect is to produce a dilution of the melanin pigments with the brown being almost completely suppressed and the black becoming a pale grey. In the Green and Agate series some interesting, and often quite beautiful, birds are to be found, such as the Green Opal, Red Agate Opal and Rose Agate Opal (a delightful pink and grey effect). Among the Browns and Isabels, however, the birds although true Selfs, appear to be almost Clear.

The opal mutation is of an ordinary recessive nature and is not sex-linked (autosomal). There is no lethal gene involved so that opals mated together will breed true and produce 100% opal young. Two non-opals, provided that they are carriers of the opal factor, can still produce some opal progeny (25%).

The table for matings involving the opal factor is as below.

OPEN SHOWS

These have already been defined under the heading of *EXHIBITIONS*.

OUTBREEDING

Outbreeding consists of breeding from unrelated stock and introducing fresh blood every year or so in order to ensure that no *INBREEDING* (which see) takes place. This system is generally held to produce more vigorous progeny but, of course, a genuine strain of birds cannot be built up in this way. Some fanciers who are not too seriously concerned with breeding theories find that outbreeding serves their purpose very well. If the initial stock and the regular replacements are of good quality, some perfectly reasonable show specimens can usually be expected, and with the occasional prospect of something even more worthwhile.

PARENTS	PROGENY
Opal x Opal	All Opal
Normal x Opal	All Normal carrying Opal
Normal carrying Opal x Normal carrying Opal	25% Normal, 50% Normal carrying Opal, 25% Opal
Normal x Normal carrying Opal	All Normal, but 50% will be carrying Opal
Opal x Normal carrying Opal	50% Opal, 50% Normal carrying Opal

Matings can be carried out either way round, as no sex-linkage is involved.

P Q

PADOVAN FRILL

This breed is a fairly recent addition to the family of frilled canaries. It is the result of the ingenuity of Italian fanciers and named after the city of Padua from which it comes. It is a largish bird of somewhat Parisian type, although it lacks some of the frilling of that breed. Additionally it has a crest on the crown of the head which distinguishes it from all other frilled varieties.

According to information available, the Padovan was created by the blending of Parisian and North Dutch blood with the crested gene being supplied by the Gloster Fancy. In Britain the Lancashire has also been used to improve the size and length of the bird while at the same time giving its own contribution to the crest.

The Padovan should stand up well and display itself in a commanding and fearless manner with the head, body and tail in line. As with other large frilled breeds, the feathering should be long and dense, with the mantle, craw and fins symmetrically arranged in the

approved manner. The crest is of the usual pattern found in all crested breeds, that is to say, circular in shape, centrally placed on top of the head, and with the broad, leafy feathers radiating evenly all round to fall well over the beak and eyes.

All of the basic canary colours are admissible although preference is always given to a bird having a crest contrasting with its body, i.e., a dark or grizzled crest on an otherwise clear body.

Like all crested breeds, the Padovan exists in both crested and plain-headed forms. They should be mated together in the usual manner of Crest x Plainhead to give the genetical expectation of 50% of each type among the progeny. The crested bird of this breed is, of course, easily recognizable by its head decoration but the plainhead might easily be confused with the other frilled breeds. The main points of difference, however, are that its head and neck should be devoid of any frilling except that the head should have distinctive overhanging eyebrows similar to the plainheads of other crested breeds.

Also, the mantle should be more like that of the North Dutch Frill, abundant and widespreading over the shoulders but without the *bouquet* (the additional rosette of feathers at the lower end of the mantle).

Official Standard

The Padovan Frill was recognized by the *C.O.M.* in 1974 and given the following standard, which differs in some respects from that of the Italian Frilled Canary authorities.

CREST — Abundant feathers, preferably of a dark colour
MANTLE — Regular, well furnished and symmetrical; with a middle parting
FLANKS — Starting from the femur on each side of the bird to rise concentrically around the wings
TAIL — Long and sturdy
COCK FEATHERS — Falling on each side of the tail

BREAST FRILLS — Abundant frills, forming a voluminous jabot
THIGHS — Feathered and 'trousered'
NAILS — Forming a corkscrew
COLOUR — Uniform
PLUMAGE — Soft and abundant
SIZE — Minimum 17cm
CARRIAGE — Proud and elegant

	Points
HEAD AND/OR CREST	15
COLOUR UNIFORM	15
PLUMAGE	10
SIZE (17cm)	10
MANTLE	10
JABOT	10
FINS	10
WINGS	5
TAIL	5
CARRIAGE	5
GENERAL CONDITION	5
Total	100

PAIRING

Pairing, in the purely physical sense of introducing the birds to each other so that breeding can proceed, has already been dealt with under *MATING*. Other aspects of the subject are systems of pairing and theoretical planning, on paper, before the breeding season begins.

Systems of pairing consist of:

1 Single pairing as already detailed under mating, i.e., the normal procedure of one cock to one hen and the pair remaining together throughout the breeding season.

2 Double pairing, where a trio of birds is used consisting of a cock bird and two hens. This is usually accomplished by allowing him to run with each of his partners alternately for a part of each day, transferring him from one to the other each morning and evening, or more often if necessary. If the two hens are not in breeding condition at the same time he can put the first hen to nest and then, while she is incubating, turn his attention to the second, later returning to the first hen to help rear the brood and put her to nest for the second time, and so on.

3 Multiple pairing, where a cock bird can be mated to a larger number of hens. In this system, he is introduced to each hen in turn as she becomes ready for nesting, but is only allowed to remain with her for a short time to permit copulation to take place. The hens are expected to sit and rear their broods on the own, which the majority quite easily do.

Of these systems, the first is the most natural and straightforward, and therefore easy to handle by the beginner in the hobby. The other two are useful in making use of an outstanding cock bird with the obvious intention of passing on his superior genes to a larger number of offspring.

Planning the pairing of one's birds is one of those winter evening exercises that are so fascinating to canary fanciers. If proper records have been kept, the pedigree and performance of each bird, both on the show bench and in any previous breeding season, can be checked. Notes will also be needed regarding the strengths and weaknesses of each bird, and it is often a good idea to give them marks, using the standard scale of points for the breed, to assist in the assessment. Armed with all of this information, it should be possible to put together the most suitable partners for the coming season, having regard to the many facets that need taking into consideration such as sex, colour, markings and degree of consanguinity.

Such is the tantilizing nature of livestock breeding, however, that with all the forward planning in the world, results are not always what one might hope for. Two otherwise admirable birds may not get on at all well together or, for some unrecognized genetical reason, do not happen to achieve the desired results whereas, given other partners, they may well produce the ideal that is being sought.

PARASITES

Canaries are liable to suffer from the attention of a number of body parasites. *LICE* were dealt with under that particular heading. The other major pest of canaries, and many other birds, is *RED MITE* (which see). In some countries, fanciers are also troubled a good deal by Northern Mite, the incidence of which may vary from season to season. All of these parasites are controllable and, if the proper treatment is applied, need never present any serious threat to the birds. Any fancier whose stock is free from parasites should never become complacent, and routine preventive measures should be taken, especially before and after the breeding season. A careful watch should also be kept upon birds that have been out to shows and to any new stock that has been introduced to the birdroom.

PARISIAN FRILL

(see colour feature page 122)

This variety has received passing mention under previous headings where reference was made to its very special position among the frilled group of breeds. This is because the Parisian is not only the largest of them all but possesses the curled feather characteristic developed to the most marked degree. An outstanding specimen appears to be almost completely covered in a mass of frills.

The breed is of quite an ancient date. It was probably developed from the old race of Frilled Canaries that spread from the Low Countries into French Flanders in the early years of the last century and thence to the capital city where a specialist society for its enthusiasts existed well before the First World War. A small booklet devoted to the breed, and entitled *Le Serin Hollandais Parisien*, was published in Paris early this century.

In general terms, the Parisian Frill is distinguished by its length of body, commanding appearance, and the aforementioned extreme development of frilling which combines to make it a very impressive bird.

In size it is the equal of the English Lancashire canary, often measuring 20 to 22cm in length (around 8in) and no show specimen should be less than 19cm. Unflighted birds may tend to be a little less than the older birds as they continue to develop well into their second year. Some birds, in fact, may not reach their peak until their third year.

The old French standard for the breed called for its carriage to be 'proud and majestic' but also allowed that 'low carriage' was permissible although the upright stance was always to have preference at shows. The modern *C.O.M.* standard merely says that the carriage may be either 'erect or crouching'. However, to see the difference between a bird that squats on its perch and one that stands boldly upright on strong legs with plenty of confidence in its bearing, is to recognize at once why earlier standards said that high carriage was to be preferred.

The frilled plumage can vary between being long, soft and wavy (soft feather) on the one hand and that which is shorter, crisper and more tightly curled (hard feather) on the other. The former adds greatly to the impression of size in the bird, with the mantle in particular giving great width across the shoulders, and the fins sweeping wide and then upwards around the wings.

In a good Parisian, the parting of the mantle should extend well down the back and end above the rump in a *bouquet*, or rosette of feathers. On the breast, too, the feathering should be quite dense and voluminous and sweep forwards and upwards under the chin to form the typical frilly shirt-front (*jabot*).

In addition to the three major frilled areas, the Parisian has an abundance of curled feathering elsewhere so that it often appears to be more or less frilled all over. The head has a hood or helmet of curled feathrs sweeping up the nape of the neck towards the crown, twisted feathers on the face forming some whiskers, and long eyebrows which may fall to one side, or on both sides of the head like those of a Crest-bred Canary.

The neck possesses a general

collar of frills and the rump and vent area (the *olive*) are also well curled and have the long upper tail coverts falling on each side of the tail in the same manner as a cock. The thighs are well covered with long, curly feathers. Another unusual feature of this breed is that the toenails may be curled, almost like a corkscrew.

All of this adds up to what is clearly a most highly developed fancy variety of canary which, unfortunately, is not always fully appreciated by those fanciers to whom anything a little out of the ordinary is viewed with disapproval.

Official Standard
The standard set for the Parisian Frill by the *C.O.M.* reads as follows:

WHISKERS

JABOT — Frills long and well furnished adorn each side of the breast and form a symmetrical jabot in the form of a shell

FINS — Parting concentrically on each side of the bird to rise upwards around the wings

OLIVE AND THIGHS — Well furnished with frills

HEAD — Bold. *Skull-cap* feathers falling on one or both side of the head. *Hood* feathers raised up and rolled forming a helmet

NECK — Well furnished

COLLERETTE — (Throat, bib, neck)

MANTLE — Feather long and well furnished which divide the back with a central and longitudinal parting to fall symmetrically on each side (wings)

BOUQUET — Continuation of the mantle; a rosette near the loins

COCK FEATHERS — Falling on each side of the tail

TAIL — Very strong and broad, ending squarely

NAILS — In the form of a corkscrew

SIZE — 19/22cm

POSITION — Erect or crouching

PLUMAGE — Long and fine or short and hard

	Points
SIZE (min. 19cm)	10
PLUMAGE	10
CARRIAGE	10
MANTLE — bouquet	10
JABOT	10
FINS	15
HEAD	6
FRILLS OF NECK	2
COCK FEATHERS	5
WINGS	5
LEGS — trousered	–
NAILS — curled	5
TAIL	4
GENERAL CONDITION	8
Total	100

PERCHES
Although a fairly obvious and simple item of birdkeeping equipment, perches need a certain amount of thought and it is quite important to get them right in order to avoid various problems that might arise. Loose-fitting perches can be the cause of infertility at breeding time, lack of confidence when undergoing training for show, and ultimately bad carriage when in the show cage itself.

The most usual way of fitting a perch is to have a small nail or panel pin at one end and a vertical notch cut in the other. The former fits into a small hole at the back of the cage, while the notch engages one of the upright wires of the cage front as the perch rests firmly on one of the crossbars. A certain amount of springiness is no bad thing and so, as an alternative, some fanciers use a twist-on type of perch which fits between the uprights but is just clear of the back of the cage.

Perches can vary in section being round, oval, rectangular or square according to choice and between about 1-2cm (⅜ and ¾in) in thickness. They should preferably be made of some kind of softwood in order not to be too hard on the birds' feet but, of course, natural perches can be cut out from any suitable trees or shrubs if desired. The plain, softwood perches, however, are easy to remove for washing and cleaning each week and it is always a good plan to have a plentiful supply of spares to place in the cages while this is taking place.

Show cage perches are usually of a size and pattern laid down in the specifications of the specialist societies and these must be adhered to if disqualification is to be avoided. Not all societies are equally demanding in this respect and if the choice of perch is left to the exhibitor they should be of a size and pattern befitting the type of bird being shown. Perches that are too thick in section should be avoided for the smaller and daintier breeds, whereas any that are too thin would be useless for any of the birds of position who need to grip the perch comfortably in order to stand up well and hold a good posture.

PET CANARY

Although this book has mainly been concerned with the canary fancier who raises birds for exhibition, it is appreciated that, in spite of the rise in popularity of the budgerigar over the past fifty years, there are still many people who keep a single canary purely as a household pet.

Along with many other species of small birds, canaries are readily available in most pet shops and so, unless a breeder can be contacted directly, it is here that a purchase is most likely to be made. The pet shop proprietor, or his assistant, will obviously try to be helpful at the prospect of making a sale but he may not necessarily be a canary specialist and so it would be sensible to take along a knowledgeable friend who would be able to note any shortcomings in the birds on offer.

It must first be pointed out that, in fact, most of the canaries that find their way into pet shops are the rejects of breeders who have not been able to dispose of them in any other way! They may merely be substandard specimens froim an exhibitor's point of view, which is no detriment in a pet bird. On the other hand, the birds may be those that are not in the best of health, which is clearly something to be avoided.

If no help is available, it is important to observe the birds carefully for a few minutes to see how they behave. Signs that they are in good health are:

1 They are lively and alert;
2 They have a clear, bright eye;
3 They fly briskly about the cage, or hop readily from perch to perch;
4 They call sharply to one another and cock birds may well be singing;
5 They have clean, tight plumage with a distinct sheen to it.

Signs of poor health in canaries are, by contrast:

1 They are listless;
2 Their eyes are dull;
3 They are lethargic in movement, often squatting down on their perches;
4 They rarely call and may have laboured breathing accompanied by a pumping of the tail;
5 They have loose, dull plumage and the feathers around the vent may be soiled.

Since it is usually only cock birds that are required as household pets on account of their song, it is obviously sensible to choose a bird actually heard singing. It is extremely difficult to sex canaries, apart from their song, and even a lifelong fancier would not claim infallibility. Some pointers are given elsewhere under the heading *SEXING*.

The question of which breed to choose is one that will probably not trouble the purchaser at all but a survey of pet shops shows that the majority that are available consist of Borders, Glosters, Fifes, Rollers or Coloured Canaries, all of which are perfectly good subjects.

Cages chosen for pet birds are usually of the open wire pattern which may either be hung up or placed upon a table. They have been designed with the pet bird market in mind and most are quite suitable for their purpose so that the pattern chosen will be a matter of personal preference. As a guide, however, the following points may be noted:

1 The cage should be of a reasonable size to allow the bird sufficient exercise;

2 It should have a draw tray that can be removed for cleaning;

3 The seed and water vessels should be of a shape that can easily be cleaned out;

4 There should be a protective screen of glass or plastic surrounding the lower half of the cage to prevent seed husks from being scattered into the room and to provide some protection from draughts.

Apart from the fixed perches, these ornamental cages are often provided with a swing which, in the case of canaries, is quite unnecessary and should be removed. Similarly the mirrors, toys and other ornaments that are supplied for budgerigars are not needed for canaries.

The worst health hazards for the pet canary are draughts and fluctuating temperatures and thus the cage should be so placed with the object of avoiding them. In most circumstances a window is the least suitable of all places for, although the presence of double-glazing would eliminate the possibility of draughts, the effects of direct sun may make the position unnecessarily hot at times. Canaries, of course, do appreciate a little sunshine but are best not exposed to direct sunlight for long periods of time.

If the bird is kept in the living room of the house it is advisable to cover the cage in the evening with a cloth so that a proper period of sleep can be enjoyed; the bird itself is usually a good indicator of when it wishes to go to roost for the night.

Reference to other sections of this book will give details of the various kinds of food suitable for canaries at different seasons of the year. These instructions can, of course, also be carried out with the single pet canary if desired but, for most owners, the simplest method is to supply one of the proprietary seed mixtures sold in packets at pet shops. This dry seed mixture will supply most of the bird's food requirements but will need to be supplemented by a little greenfood and/or seeding weeds and grasses as they become available, two or three times a week. As with exhibition breeding stock, fresh, clean water is essential and should be attended to daily. The canary will also need a piece of *CUTTLEFISH* bone attached to the wires of the cage and a supply of *GRIT* in a small pot. (See entries on both of these.)

The cage should be cleaned out at least twice a week and this is quickly done by withdrawing the sand tray, emptying the contents, and putting in a clean covering of sand. The use of sanded sheets makes the job easier still. These can be purchased to the size of the draw tray. They have the additional advantage of not sticking to the bird's feet as grains of loose sand may do in certain circumstances. At least weekly, the bird can be allowed a bath and, at the same time, the perches can be washed and replaced. Strong disinfectants should not be used for this purpose as they may be the cause of sore feet and eyes.

One minor problem for pet bird owners is the period of the moult and it can even be the cause of some concern if not properly understood. It is a natural phenomenon for canaries to renew their feathers, sometime between mid-summer and mid-autumn, and so this is only to be expected and need cause no alarm. Individual birds may vary in how long the process will take to complete but, if in good health, it should occupy no more than about six to eight weeks. During this period it must also be expected for cock birds to cease singing and they will not recommence until their moult has finished.

Any casting of feathers out of the normal moulting season may be an indication of *soft moult*. This is a sporadic, or a continuous, shedding of feathers which is often brought about by unnaturally long periods of artificial lighting, too warm an atmosphere, or various other reasons. It is often quite difficult to arrest once it has started and will keep the pet bird off song more or less permanently. A change of conditions from those causative ones mentioned above, plus a little soft food offered daily, may bring about a successful end to the condition. Special soft moult tonics for adding to the bird's water can also be obtained from pet shops and veterinary suppliers.

PIN FEATHERS

This is a fancier's term for feathers that have not yet emerged from their quills, thus giving the appearance of small, spiky pins. They are most in evidence at the close of the moult around the bird's face and head (the last parts of the body to be moulted) and, in the early part of the show season, birds often appear before the judge that are still a bit pinny. This, naturally, counts against them to some extent and often an otherwise excellent bird may fail to win a coveted special, or even a first prize, because it is not quite finished. It may then go on, later in the season, to have an all-conquering show career.

PINK-EYED

Already dealt with under the headings of *CINNAMON* and *EYE COLOUR*, in this mutation, the pink eye colour becomes darker in colour until, at maturity, it appears quite dark and is almost impossible to distinguish from a normal dark-eyed bird. Some fanciers claim to be able to do so, but probably much depends upon one's eyesight and powers of perception! If the bird happens to have markings of any kind, these will, of course, consist of the brown pigment only.

PLAINHEAD

This term means just what it says, namely, a bird with a plain head as distinct from one with a crest. There is no need to use the term at all, of course, in connection with most breeds of canary where crests are not a feature. In the past it was used in the Norwich canary fancy to distinguish the Norwich Plainhead from the Crested Norwich but nowadays the two breeds have moved apart and are

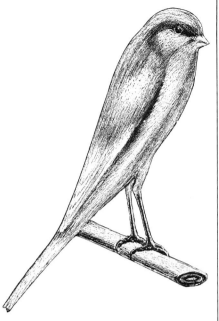

Three well-known breeds showing a variety of positions: Yorkshire (upright); Border Fancy (semi upright); Norwich Plainhead (low)

generally known simply as the Norwich, and the Crested Canary. In Britain, the Norwich Canary specialist societies still retain the word in their official titles, e.g., the Southern Norwich Plainhead Canary Club.

The non-crested bird in the Lancashire breed is also known as the Lancashire Plainhead to distinguish it from the crested form (the Lancashire Coppy).

The reader is reminded once again that, genetically, a mating of Plainhead x Plainhead will produce *only* Plain-headed progeny, whereas Plainhead x Crest gives 50% plainheads and 50% crested birds.

POSITION

Most breeds have a characteristic carriage, or manner of bearing, in some of which it is of the utmost importance. Many of the old canary handbooks, for instance, dealt with these breeds under a group heading which they specifically called 'birds of position' to emphasize an upright, or nearly upright, position. They include the Yorkshire, Lancashire and Scotch Fancy among British breeds and the Belgian, Parisian Frill and several others among those from Continental Europe.

Most other breeds of canary adopt a more normal semi-upright posture of between 40 and 60 degrees from the horizontal and a few, like the Crested Canary, stand very low across the perch at only about 30 degrees. Birds, of course, being very active creatures, do not maintain the same precise position all of the time and it would be quite unnatural to expect them to do so. *Position* refers to the typical posture that a well-trained show bird should adopt when under inspection by the judge.

If the breeder has any birds that do not readily conform to this, or which constantly resort to a slovenly squatting down, or lying across the perch, they are best excluded from any breeding plans. Bad carriage can easily be bred into a stud and is one of the most obvious and damaging faults in any show bird.

PROTEINS

These food substances are essential for proper growth and for the repair of body tissues that are constantly being worn away as the result of ordinary day-to-day activities. They are obviously important in the diet of all living creatures at all times but particularly so for canaries during the breeding and moulting seasons. Most fanciers give very little thought to the matter since proteins are generally present, in sufficient quantity, in the diets normally used.

The various breeding, rearing and moulting foods offered for sale by reputable seedsmen and birdfood specialists have been scientifically compounded and contain the correct balance of carbohydrates, fats and proteins, usually with added vitamins and minerals, so that the average fancier has no problems on that score. Those who like to make up their own foods, however, might wish to note that such items as eggs, milk, dried yeast, wholemeal and oatmeal are reliable sources of protein that can be incorporated into various types of soft food for canaries.

QUALITY

This expression is often used by canary fanciers in appraising the merits of a bird, sometimes in a limited sense by applying it to feather quality in particular and sometimes in reference to the more general all-round excellence of the bird. Quite clearly, it is not too difficult to follow what is intended by the general context of the conversation that is taking place. In any case, a beginner in the hobby should not be afraid to ask a more experienced fancier to point out exactly what he means since quality is something that is not easily described and yet readily recognized by the connoisseur. In due course, the novice will soon begin to pick up the finer points of difference which mark out the excellent bird from the more average specimen.

R

RAPE SEED

In many countries fanciers regard this as the second most important seed to canary seed as a component in the birds' diet. For this reason it commonly appears in basic staple mixtures for canaries and, during the winter months, a mixture of three parts of canary seed to one part of rape is the standard offering in the seed hoppers. Rape also figures prominently, along with teazle, hemp (in some countries), and some other seeds, in soaked seed mixtures during the breeding season. Various forms of rape seed are normally offered for sale in most seedsmen's lists, usually red rape, black rape and Rubsen rape. The older handbooks on canaries always recommended red rape, which they called alternatively summer rape, as opposed to black rape, which was winter rape. However, agricultural practices are different nowadays and very often the red rape that is now offered is the same as black rape but has merely been treated to alter its colour; this, of course, might differ according to the country of origin and the laws relating to the treatment of seeds for livestock. Rubsen rape is a different crop, grown in Germany and some other European countries, and is widely favoured by Roller Canary breeders.

REARING

The early part of the breeding season, consisting of pairing up, nest building, egg laying, incubation and hatching, is normally a reasonably trouble-free period for the fancier. Rearing, on the other hand, can be an anxious time and often is beset with problems. In fact, some older fanciers will make the distinction, somewhat ironically, between the number of birds they have bred (meaning hatched) and the number reared (i.e., brought to maturity), the two figures sometimes bearing no comparison!

If the period from hatching to weaning is taken as a more limited definition of rearing, the following points will need to be considered:

1 The ability and willingness of the parent birds to rear their own offspring;
2 Correct feeding during this period;
3 Any other problems that might possibly arise.

The first point has been discussed under the headings *FEEDERS* and *HAND REARING* where it was, nevertheless, made clear that by far the greater number of canaries make perfectly satisfactory parents and give their owners no trouble at all. Although the beginner in the hobby will be anxious to know how things are going, he should not be unduly interfering but allow his birds the chance to perform their duties and so prove themselves one way or the other.

The basic foods required for rearing canaries consist of:

1 Soft food, which is normally egg food, although some fanciers also use milksop in addition;
2 Soaked seed;
3 Wild seeds;
4 Greenfood.

All of these items are dealt with at the appropriate point in this book. Detailed articles on the raising of canaries usually appear in the columns of magazines devoted to the hobby and from these it will be noted that it is only in details concerning methods of preparation, quantities used, and at what stage the various foods are given, that fanciers may differ in their opinions.

Problems unconnected with either of those covered in the two preceding paragraphs may be:

1 Chicks falling or, more often, being accidentally pulled out of the nest;
2 The condition known as sweating;

Roller Canary

Badge of the National Roller Canary Society, one of many Roller Canary societies

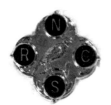

Right: Self Green Roller Canaries are still thought by some fanciers to produce the purest song

(Photograph by Cyril Laubscher)

Examples of Roller Canaries from early in this century. These are bred for song only, type and colour being immaterial

(Photograph by Cyril Laubscher)

Modern Roller Canary. When in song, the throat will be remarkably distended to give the quality of tone produced by this breed

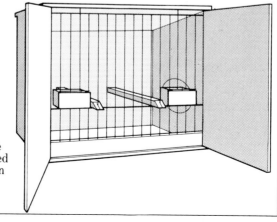

Roller Canary contest cage. The shutters are closed to keep the bird in darkness until required to sing

American Singer Canary feeding her chicks

but a sufficient quantity will be passed on to the tiny chicks. From the fourth day onwards a spray of seeding chickweed can be offered daily, if available, and from the fifth day soaked seeds. From this time all of these items should be made available to the breeding pair, the actual quantities being adjusted according to which items seem to find most favour. Individual hens may show quite marked preferences, by ignoring certain foods completely while concentrating upon others, but most of them will feed all that is offered to them.

Fanciers usually try to arrange for three feeds a day to be given so that the substances provided are always fresh. Certain items tend to turn sour fairly quickly in hot weather. It is therefore important that anything that remains uneaten from the previous feed should be removed from the cage at each feeding time; this is particularly important for those fanciers who make use of bread and milk as part of their rearing diet. The receptacles that are used for food should also receive frequent washing and sterilizing; certainly not less than once each day.

If they are well reared, canary chicks grow rapidly and should leave the nest at around 19 to 21 days old. In these circumstances, fanciers usually like to wean them from their parents, although some prefer to leave them a little longer but all young canaries should be independent by the time they are a month old. The subject of *WEANING*, its methods and problems, is dealt with under that heading.

The post-weaning period may also see some losses among the young stock so that, as stated before, the number of birds reared to maturity and finally brought through the moult as unflighted birds, may bear no resemblance to the numbers hatched. An average expectation, taken over a number of years from a single pair raising two broods, may perhaps be five youngsters per pair. Anything above this may be regarded as

3 Plucking.

The first of these happens when the hen carelessly, or hurriedly, leaves the nest, generally during the first day or two of the chicks' lives when they are quite tiny. It is less common later on when they tend to cling together in a little ball and are not so easily dislodged. If a tiny, cold, and apparently lifeless chick is discovered on the floor of the cage, it should be warmed in the hands for a few minutes and, if it then starts to wriggle, it can be put back in the nest when the chances are that it will recover. The problem of a hen plucking her own young when ready to go to next again is dealt with under *PLUCKING*, while the condition known as *SWEATING* is treated later on.

Although individual fanciers tend to have their own favourite methods of rearing, as stated above, it is usually only in minor matters that they tend to differ. A fairly common system, however, give or take a day or so either way, is to give egg food only for the first two days after hatching and on the third day to offer, in addition, a little green food such as cress or lettuce. Probably the parent birds will consume most of this at first

exceptional while, even if the average drops as low as three, most fanciers would be reasonably satisfied. There are, of course, occasional very good years when the production may be quite high, especially where three broods are taken, but most fanciers will also have experienced the disappointment of breeding seasons that have gone wrong for no accountable reason and with little to show for their efforts at the end.

RECESSIVE WHITE

Elsewhere in this book the nature of the Dominant White is dealt with and it was pointed out that most of the White Canaries found in the type breeds are representative of this mutation. The Recessive White comes more within the province of the breeder of Coloured Canaries.

The mutation occurred in the year 1908 simultaneously in England and New Zealand. Subsequently the English strain died out but, fortunately, the New Zealand one persisted so that all of the Recessive Whites of today are descendants of the New Zealand mutation. Paradoxically, until recently, this mutation was known in continental Europe as the English White!

Genetically, this variety behaves differently from the Dominant White and, upon close inspection, it can also be distinguished visually. Dominant Whites always show just a tinge of yellow pigment on the outer edges of the primary flight feathers, whereas the Recessives are devoid of any trace of lipochrome at all.

When mated together White x White, Recessive Whites breed true and produce 100% White progeny — there being no lethal gene involved as in the case of the Dominant White. Because of the recessive nature of the mutation, if a Recessive White is mated to a canary of normal colouring, no White progeny can be produced. The offspring of such a mating, however, will be carriers and, if intermated or back-crossed to Recessive Whites, can breed more Recessive Whites in the next generation.

If any melanin pigment is present, it will appear as either Blue or Fawn just as in the case of the Dominant White birds.

RED CANARY

(see colour feature pages 62-63)

In English speaking countries, the term 'Red *Factor* Canary' has persisted over the years for this new breed following the view of pioneer breeders that a red 'factor' (i.e., a gene responsible for red colouring) could be added to the canary's genetic make-up to produce a red canary. The theory was that this red gene could be transferred to the canary from the *HOODED SISKIN* (which see) through the medium of fertile hybrids which had been proved on many occasions. Unfortunately, it turned out that there was no such thing as this theoretical red factor but that red colouring was produced by the combination of several inter-acting genes, plus certain essential food substances in the birds' diet.

During the 1930s many years of painstaking work took place which was repeated and followed up after the Second World War. This involved the careful selection of the best birds from experimental matings and back-crossing them to Hooded Siskins. This was not made any easier by the fact that, in the earlier generations, there was a lot of infertility, especially among the hens. However, that is all in the past and today's fancier has been left the legacy of canaries that are not far short of red. They form an important section of our shows.

It must be pointed out, however, that these birds still owe much of their brilliant colouring to the use of a preparation of canthaxanthin at moulting time. Without it they are still not much better than orange. Nevertheless, they are extremely attractive and eye-catching birds, well worth the consideration of any newcomer to the hobby when deciding which breed to take up.

As with all other canaries, there

Crested Canary

Variegated
Crested Canary
with untidy crest
feathers which will
form a more
perfect shape when
it has completed its
moult

(Photograph by Cyril Laubscher)

118

An early illustration from "Our Canaries" of a pair of Crested Canaries. Clear birds like these are now rarely found in this breed

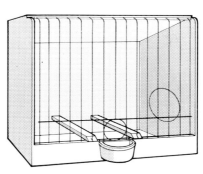

Crested Canary show cage which has widely spaced bars and a large drinker hole to prevent damage to the bird's crest

Left: Crest-Bred Canary showing the broad head and overhanging eyebrows required of this type

graph by Cyril Laubscher)

Player's Cigarettes

Clear Crest-Bred Canary

are the usual two feather types to be found which, in this case, are called intensive (the Yellow, or Non-frosted bird) and Non-intensive (the Buff or Frosted). Older fanciers sometimes persist with the terms Red-orange and Apricot, which are now obsolete, the latter being particularly inappropriate nowadays since the birds are nothing like the colour of an apricot!

Red Canaries are usually exhibited as clear birds, although marked and variegated specimens are permitted and sometimes may have classes to themselves at the larger shows. In the Self form, in combination with the various melanin pigments and their mutations, the Red Canary produces some of the most beautiful of all coloured canaries. An unusual feature of the red pigmentation is that it is only to be seen at its best in natural daylight. In most show halls, unfortunately, this is not possible and so the artificial lighting, especially of the fluorescent type, inhibits viewing the glowing red colour of the birds.

During the experimental years, type was regarded as irrelevant and the birds developed in a rather haphazard fashion into a nondescript form which owed much to the Siskins and Roller Canaries in their ancestry. Today, as a result of standards laid down by the specialist societies, the type has been much improved. The ideal is largely based upon that of the Border and Fife Fancies but, in size, is somewhere midway between the two.

RED MITE
This pest has always constituted one of the major problems for bird keepers although today's fancier, being more aware of the importance of hygiene, is far less troubled than were his predecessors. In fact, the conscientious breeder makes it a matter of routine to ensure that these parasites are unknown in his birdroom.

Red mites are so called because they appear to be red, due to the blood that has been sucked from the body of their host, although they are actually grey in colour when unfed. They do not have permanent residence upon the body of the bird, but during the daytime hide away in cracks and crevices to come out at night to attack their victims. During warm weather they reproduce very rapidly and so, in summer, a severe infestation can rapidly build up unless a sharp lookout is kept.

Their presence can be detected by examining likely hiding places such as the ends of perches, corners of cages, joints in the woodwork, spaces between wire fronts and supporting bars, and even inside the seed hoppers. As mentioned above, they will appear as tiny red specks but, if they have become well established, there will also be a lot of greyish detritus matter around.

They are not rapid movers like lice and so they can easily be destroyed by treating them, and the areas that they occupy, with a suitable insecticide. An old fanciers' remedy was to dissolve some camphor in paraffin or turpentine and then to paint this on all of the likely cracks and crevices where the pest might reside. Nowadays aerosol sprays for treating insect pests are available from pet shops but it is important to get one that is designed for birdroom use.

Although one's birdroom and cages may be clear of parasites, it must not be assumed that they will always remain so, as a short while off guard may allow the introduction of this pest. The greatest source of contamination is probably at shows where one's cages and travelling cases may be placed next to some others whose owners have not been so particular. Also, any new birds introduced into the birdroom should be isolated for a while until it is certain that they are free from trouble. Although the mites do not permanently reside upon the body of a bird, there is always the danger that a few might have come along for the ride!

RINGING

If proper breeding records are to be kept, it is essential that all birds should have identification rings upon their legs. It may be possible, where a small stock is kept, to memorize the pedigree of the birds but it becomes increasingly difficult after a couple or so generations have gone by. There are two kinds of rings — split and closed rings. The former are in widespread use throughout the fancy and the latter are insisted upon in Europe and USA and by one or two specialist societies in other countries.

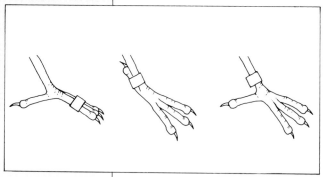

The three stages in close ringing

Split rings can be put on at any time but it is usual to do so when the young birds are first taken from their parents before transferring them to stock or flight cages. These rings are made of a light plastic material, available in a variety of colours and numbered consecutively. They can be opened at the split using a special expanding tool. The ring is then easily slipped over the shank of the bird's leg and the tool withdrawn, thus leaving the ring behind encircling the leg.

Closed rings can only be put on when the chicks are quite small, usually at five or six days old, otherwise their feet will have grown too big to go through the ring. To do this, the front three toes are brought together and the ring passed over them, then back over the ball of the foot and over the back toe which has been held close to the shank of the leg. When the ring is clear and on the shank, the hind toe is allowed to resume its normal position.

Many fanciers do not like to use this latter method because some hens seem to object to the rings, especially those of the bright aluminium kind, and try to remove them with obviously detrimental results to the chicks. However, it is clear that closed rings are the only real guarantee of a bird's parentage since, unlike the split rings, they cannot be removed and replaced at will.

Whichever method is chosen it is essential to make an immediate note of colour, number, parentage, date of hatching and any other relevant information that may be necessary for the records.

ROLLER CANARY

The culture of the Roller is a very specialized branch of the canary fancy which will appeal especially to those who have a good musical ear. All of the other breeds are essentially visual in their attraction by reason of their shape, posture, colour, markings and so on, but the Roller is bred purely for its singing ability. Its physical appearance counts for nothing to the real connoisseur of the breed.

The origin of these specialized songsters dates back as far as the eighteenth century when the domestic canary first received the attention of fanciers in the Hartz Mountains region of Germany. So successful was their application to the matter that the Hartz Mountain Roller Canary soon became the most desirable acquisition of fanciers throughout Europe where, today, they are still more widely bred than the type canaries in many countries.

Over the years the song of the Roller has become as far removed from that of the wild canary as the appearance of the Parisian Frill differs from the small greenish wild birds of the islands. It has been arrived at by an equally long period of selection.

The Roller's song is delivered through an almost closed beak and comes from deep within the throat. It is much quieter than the normal canary's song and consists of a continuous trilling and warbling that rises and falls in pitch and is delivered in such a varying manner

(see colour feature pages 114-115)

Parisian Frill

The Parisian Frill shows the most intense development of frilling including the head, neck, rump and thighs. Another feature of this breed is curled toenails

(Photograph by Cyril Laubscher)

Official standard illustration of a Parisian Frill showing all the frilling that is required

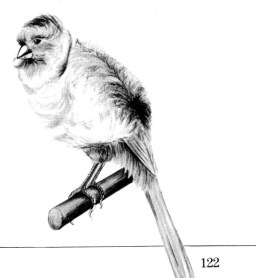

Far Right: All frilled canaries are exhibited in open wire cages which show the bird to its best advantage

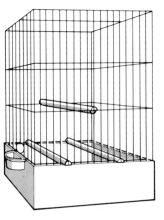

North Dutch Frill

A North Dutch Frill as depicted in "Our Canaries"

Player's Cigarettes

Dutch Frill Canary

A Dutch Frill Canary showing additional frilling which is a fault in this variety

The North Dutch Frill should exhibit the three basic frills only, with the head, neck and lower parts of the body having no frills

(Photograph by Cyril Laubscher)

that the experts have recognized and named fourteen different song passages. These are divided into two groups, the *rolls* being sung at a very fast tempo, as in a drum roll, and the *tours* with a more emphatic beat. Not all birds of the breed are capable of rendering all the song passages, any more than a bird of one of the type breeds is likely to excel in every point, but in any case the quality of the performance, rather than mere variety, is regarded as of greater importance.

For the Roller fancier, careful selection of the most promising songsters, plus a rigorous training programme under the tuition of a proved performer, is essential for success at the song contests where these birds are marked on a points system. During their performance the judge listens carefully to each bird and allocates marks for each of the song passages as they are delivered, according to the excellence of the singer. At the same time points may be deducted for any faults in the way of harsh notes, long pauses or undesirable interjections.

Although something of a minority interest, the Roller fancy has its dedicated devotees. Since Rollers are never shown at the normal mixed open shows, to avoid them picking up any harsh singing notes from the other canaries, the type and song sections of the canary fancy tend not to meet.

ROSE

When dealing with the various ground colours of the canary this particular colour form was briefly mentioned. The mutation was originally called the *lipochrome pastel* on account of its effect upon the ground colour which was to dilute the yellow or, in this case the red, into a pastel shade throughout. It will be recalled from the earlier reference mentioned that the yellow lipochrome becomes the Ivory and the red becomes Rose.

In its clear form the Rose can be of a delightful shade of wild rose pink although, these days, many tend to be more of a salmon colour. Clear Rose birds can easily be bred along with any normal stock of Red Canaries. The mutation being recessive and sex-linked has a similar mode of inheritance to that of the Cinnamon to Green and a table of breeding expectations accompanies this note.

Self birds with the rose ground colour can be very attractive indeed, examples being the Rose Agate, Rose Isabel and Rose Opal among others.

THE EXPECTATION FROM RED AND ROSE MATINGS

	PARENTS	PROGENY
1	Red cock x Red hen	All Red
2	Rose cock x Rose hen	All Rose
3	Red cock x Rose hen	Red hens. Red cocks carrying Rose
4	Rose cock x Red hen	Red cocks carrying Rose, Rose hens
5	Red cock carrying Rose x Red hen	Red cocks, Red cocks carrying Rose, Red hens, Rose hens
6	Red cock carrying Rose x Rose hen	Red cocks carrying Rose, Rose cocks, Red hens, Rose hens

In the table, birds labelled Red and Rose for simplicity, may be either intensive or non-intensive. Normally all of the matings would be of the usual intensive x non-intensive variety.

S

instead of darkening as does the pink eye of the Cinnamon (brown). (See also *INO*.)

Genetically, this mutation, like so many others, is a sex-linked recessive and thus follows the familiar pattern in breeding, the full table being set out below.

SATINETTE

The Satinette is one of the more recent mutations in the realm of colour breeding, having occurred during the late 1960s but not being readily available to fanciers generally for several years after that. As mentioned elsewhere, the breeding of the newer colour mutations is something of a specialized field for the canary fancier and possibly nowhere is this more so than in the case of the Satinette. This is because the effects of the mutation are variable according to the basic colours with which it is associated, e.g., Agate Satinette, Red Orange Isabel Satinette, Rose Brown Satinette, Silver Isabel Satinette.

All traces of eumelanin black pigment are removed from the feather by this mutation but, in some cases, the brown melanin that remains is practically invisible so that the bird appears as a clear. In others, the striations on the back and flanks may be either faint and narrow or wide and heavy. One constant feature of the satinette series, however, is that all birds possess a bright red eye which persists into adulthood

SCOTCH FANCY

This is one of the classical ornamental fancy varieties that were so popular in Britain during Victorian times, especially with fanciers in Scotland, hence the name of the breed. Its history goes as far back as the 1820s where its origins lay in Belgian stock. Half a century later, it had achieved an immense following, particularly in and around the city of Glasgow. Later in the century, attempts at improvement led to extensive crossbreeding with the (by then) highly developed Belgian Canary. This practice proved to be detrimental to the breed's fortunes for, not only did it begin to bear a considerable resemblance to the Belgian itself, but a gradual decline from popular favour also occurred and has continued until recent times.

Since 1970, with the re-awakening of interest in the old varieties of canary, there has been a heartening revival in the fortunes of the Scotch Fancy and there is now every chance of a good recovery. Although possibly not to be recommended for a beginner, the Scotch Fancy of today is a

(see colour feature pages 82-83)

THE EXPECTATIONS FROM SATINETTE MATINGS

	PARENTS	PROGENY
1	Satinette cock x Satinette hen	All Satinette
2	Normal cock x Satinette hen	Normal hens, normal cocks carrying Satinette
3	Satinette cock x normal hen	Normal cocks carrying Satinette, Satinette hens
4	Normal cock carrying Satinette x normal hen	Normal cocks, normal cocks carrying Satinette, normal hens, Satinette hens
5	Normal cock carrying Satinette x Satinette hen	Normal cocks carrying Satinette, Satinette, Satinette cocks, normal hens, Satinette hens

Belgian Canary

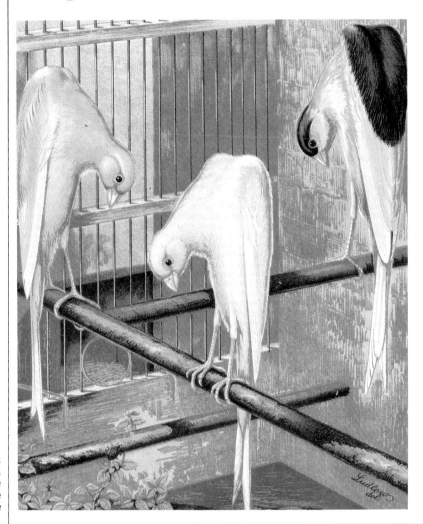

Belgian Canaries in the nineteenth century when the breed was at the height of its fame

The Confederation Ornithologique Mondiale is an organisation which co-ordinates the standards and exhibiting of canaries, including the two breeds illustrated, in many European countries

Belgian Canary of the present day

(Photograph by Cyril Laubscher)

Gibber Italicus

(Photograph by Cyril Laubscher)

The Gibber Italicus
is one of the
strangest of all
frilled breeds with
its sparse
feathering and
exaggerated
posture

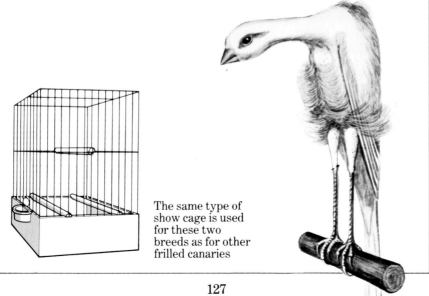

The same type of
show cage is used
for these two
breeds as for other
frilled canaries

The standard
illustration of the
ideal Gibber
Italicus

relatively free and easy breeder so that anyone desirous of taking up something out of the ordinary could try their hand with it.

This variety is another of those breeds in which type and position play an essential part in producing the ideal for which enthusiasts aim. Since 1970 this has involved a return to earlier standards that prevailed before outcrossing with the Belgian took place, so that the modern Scotch Fancy should follow the same lines as its ancestors of a century ago. This calls for a long, slim bird which has a pronounced curve to its body so that, in show posture with its head thrust well forward and tail carried under the perch, the general outline is in the form of a crescent moon. Generally speaking, the greater the curvature displayed, the more highly the bird is regarded. It should also show plenty of agility in its movement from perch to perch, bouncing across on supple legs and with the tail swinging freely instead of being rigidly held as in most other breeds.

The head of the Scotch Fancy should be oval and sleek, its neck long and fine and capable of being extended with plenty of drive or reach when the bird is in position. The body, from the shoulders and breast downwards should be a long, slim and tapering curve with the feathering being as smooth as possible, although this latter point is subordinate to the more important characteristics of the curved posture. Some of the very best birds in fact, do carry some excess feather at the waist and on the shoulder. This is a failing inherited from some of their ancestors in whose day shape and posture was everything and feather quality counted for nothing.

Official Standard

The standard for exhibition Scotch Fancies is as follows:

Points

SHAPE — Body long and tapering and curved in the form of a half circle, convex above, concave below, with a clean outline, feather being close, short and tight 20

HEAD AND NECK — small, neat snaky head. Long, tapering neck 10

SHOULDERSS AND BACK — High, narrow, rounded shoulders, well filled in. Long, narrow, well-filled back, curving from shoulders to tail 20

TAIL — Long, narrow, closely folded and well curved under the perch 5

STYLE, NERVE AND TRAVELLING — Well raised up, forming a high circle. Bold, free and jaunty carriage with plenty of life and action 25

SIZE — Approximately 6¾in (17cm) 10

QUALITY AND CONDITION — Clean, healthy, perfect condition 10

Total 100

SELF

Under earlier headings the term *SELF* has already been defined but, for the sake of ready reference it is repeated here. A Self bird is one in which the melanin (dark) pigments are present throughout the plumage, with no light feathers appearing anywhere to break its solidity. White feathers in the wings or tail will render the bird Foul and a small amount of light feathering on the body as well will constitute a Three Parts Dark.

According to the type of ground colour, and the presence of one or both of the melanins, a self bird may be a Self Green, Self Cinnamon, Self Blue, Self Fawn and so on. In the Coloured Canary section of the fancy the number of different Selfs are too numerous to list here and it is interesting to note that in some of the mutations the melanins are so altered by dilution that, at a casual glance, the birds may have the appearance of Clears. Only an examination of the underflue will show that of the Self to be pale beige whereas that of the genuine Clear will be white.

SEXING

The canary is a species in which there is no very well marked difference between the sexes, but familiarity with his stock will soon enable the new fancier to notice the subtle differences between the cocks and hens.

To begin with there will be no difficulty since the initial stock, purchased with a reputable fancier, will already be sexed and the cocks and hens will have been pointed out to him. As the breeding season approaches the most obvious differences will become apparent — that of song. In the canary, the cocks sing, whereas the hens do not. Occasionally one comes across singing hens and some cock birds are rather reluctant songsters. Nevertheless, the presence or absence of song is a 98 per cent guide to sex in adult birds.

Song also helps with the sexing of the young stock of the year for, although the newly-weaned youngsters may all look alike, by the time they are around eight to ten weeks old, most of the cocks will have started to twitter. It will not be like the loud full-throated song of the adult cocks, but a soft, continuous singing which is quite unmistakable if they are carefully observed.

Although most of the cocks will have started singing at about this time, it should be borne in mind that not all of the non-singers will definitely turn out to be hens. It has been the experience of most fanciers to have the occasional bird, that has been completely silent throughout the winter months, suddenly to start singing when spring comes around, and so an otherwise excellent hen turns out to be a cock bird after all!

Apart from the song, there are two other methods of sexing used by fanciers. These are colour and general bearing, and the appearance of the sex organs at breeding time.

Colour. Cocks are mainly more intense in colour than their counterparts, e.g., a yellow cock is of a deeper and richer yellow than a yellow hen; a buff cock shows more colour and has less dense frosting than a buff hen. This may be rather difficult to assess just by looking at an individual bird but, by comparison with a similar bird

of known sex, the difference will become apparent. It will also be observed that cock birds tend to have a bolder manner and more jaunty carriage than hens — again quite a subtle distinction, but detectable with experience.

Sex organs. Birds have no distinctly different sex organs like mammals but, when in breeding condition, if the vent area is examined it will be seen that the cloaca of the cock bird is quite prominent and somewhat elongated. In the hen, although it is raised above the general level of the abdomen, it is rounder and flatter. This difference, it must be emphasized, is only apparent when the birds are in full breeding condition and cannot be used as a guide to sex at other periods of the year.

As a footnote it may be added that, in the realms of colour breeding where certain sex-linked matings are involved, it is possible to differentiate between the sexes of the young because of the colours involved (see following note).

SEX-LINKED

Several of the mutations in the canary are of the sex-linked variety. In other words, the transference of the gene and its visible expression are dependent upon the sex of the birds involved. In the section on *GENETICS*, it was explained that the chromosomes which determine the sex of an individual are known by the letters X and Y and that, in birds, the cock has two X chromosomes and the hen has one X and one Y. When these two chromosomes pair off randomly during fertilization, two Xs may come together, thus producing a male, or an X may pair with a Y to produce a female.

The Y chromosome, in fact, is merely rudimentary and only carries the genes for femaleness, whereas the X chromosome has, among other things, the genes for the melanin pigments. From this it follows that any recessive mutations in these pigments will need the gene to be present on both chromosomes in the cock bird, but only on the one in the hen, for it to be visibly expressed. An example of this is in the early mutant form, the Cinnamon (brown), which was shown diagrammatically in the section on genetics.

Some other sex-linked characteristics are the Agate, Isabel, Lipochrome Pastel (Ivory and Rose), Melanin Pastel and Satinette. Non sex-linked mutations include the crest and frills, Dominant White, Recessive White, Opal and Ino.

SHOWING
Under *EXHIBITING* some of the general issues concerning this aspect of the hobby were mentioned. Here the more practical aspects of the subject will be dealt with and these may, perhaps, best be resolved under the following sub-headings:

1 Show Cages
Unlike the exhibiting of pigeons, poultry, rabbits, etc., where the show authorities provide the pens in which the exhibits are to be staged, in Britain the canary fancier is obliged to provide his own show cages. Unfortunately, these are quite expensive items although, if the fancier is also a good craftsman, it is quite permissible for him to make his own — provided that the specifications laid down by the specialist society are strictly adhered to. The whole point is that all of the birds should be shown in identical cages so that neither advantage nor disadvantage should accrue in any way as a result of non-conformity. Although show cages have come in for criticism now and again, they have stood the test of time having, in most part, been designed, or at least approved by the relevant specialist societies many years ago.

2 Show training
Show training starts when the young birds of the year have been weaned and have settled down to life in their stock cages

— say at the age of about six weeks. It begins by merely hanging a show cage on to their stock cage, both doors being open, so that they can explore and become accustomed to the new cage. Later, the show cage can be gently removed with the youngster inside it for a few minutes each day, gradually increasing the time until the bird is quite happy to remain there without becoming unsettled. In some countries, it is illegal to confine a bird in a show cage for training for a period exceeding one hour in any 24 hour period. When the moult commences, many fanciers suspend any further training and take it up again more seriously when the moult has finished.

If it has already become familiar with, and quite confident in, its show cage it can easily be taught to run in, usually with the aid of a thin training stick which is gently used to guide the bird in the right direction. Eventually, it will hop inside obediently by itself as soon as the show cage is presented to it.

The later, and more exacting, stages of training consist of accustoming the bird to being handled (i.e., having its cage moved about) and to showing itself off to full advantage. All of this requires a fair amount of time and patience devoted to it,

(Photographed by Cage and Aviary)

Young birds undergoing training

although some birds are natural showmen and need less time spent on them than others may do. The degree of training needed will, therefore, vary according to the response of each individual. Any particularly nervous bird will need careful handling, otherwise it may have its show career ruined at the outset.

After the young birds have been taught to enter their show cages on demand, and they are accustomed to it being taken away and placed elsewhere in the room, the procedure usually adopted by most fanciers runs, more or less on the following lines:

a Change the position of the cage in the room from time to time so that the birds become used to having moved from place to place as it will be at a show;

b Lift the cage up in the the hand to eye level and gain the bird's confidence by quietly talking to it, or perhaps giving it a small titbit such as a spray of greenfood;

c Make the trainee become alert when its cage is being examined by gently scratching the base of the cage with the fingernail, or lightly tapping the wires;

d Encourage it to move briskly from perch to perch by means of a slight movement of the hand or training stick;

e Try to pose it for a few moments at at a time in its typical show position, again by use of the hand or the training stick. This phase of training is especially important in all of those breeds where posture is a major requirement, but even the heavier breeds such as the Norwich and Crested canary should be bright and attentive, never dull and slovenly.

Naturally, the fancier will use any or all of these training devices according to his own experience and the degree of response of his birds.

At any training session it is, of course, an advantage to deal with several birds at a time, taking each one in rotation and placing it back on the table when finished with. The lessons should be short in duration but repeated fairly often to begin with, say once or twice daily, until it becomes obvious that the birds know what is expected of them. After this, it may be necessary to exercise them only once or twice a week and, after they have been out to their first show, any further training should be unnecessary.

3 **Show preparations**

Show preparation consists of preparing birds and cages for competition. In the case of the birds, once they have been properly trained, little more needs to be done apart from keeping them immaculately clean and tight in feather. This can be achieved by the frequent use of the bath and the addition of a small teaspoonful of condition seed daily to the diet. Some fanciers also like to spray their birds from time to time with soft, clean rainwater, provided that it is free from any possible source of pollution. Others believe in giving tonics in the drinking water in the way of vitamin and mineral additives but, with sound and healthy stock maintained in hygienic conditions, a plain and wholesome diet is well suited to keeping the birds in hard condition. The possible need for occasional *HANDWASHING* has already been mentioned and, in the case of older birds, their toenails (and possibly beaks) may also need trimming (see *TOENAILS*).

Show cages should be in perfect order. A newcomer to the fancy, of course, is likely to have purchased new ones which will therefore present no problem, but occasionally a judge will encounter birds in cages that are not only shabby, but not even clean. Such a lack of care and thought on the part of the exhibitor is to be deplored, for a decent bird deserves to be well shown. It is appreciated that a judge is there to judge the birds and not the cages but, in the case of two exhibits being of equal merit, obviously he is going to favour the one whose owner has gone to the trouble of staging the bird to the best of his or her ability.

One final point for the exhibitor is to ensure that his show cage labels are securely stuck on, and in the correct place. This may vary from country to country, and there may be variations from the norm in the case of certain specialist societies, whose rules should be consulted.

SILVER

As in the case of the term Gold, there are two different applications of this form of nomenclature. In the case of the Lizard Canary, it is the Buff, or Frosted, bird of the breed — the older name of the Silver having been retained for this truly ancient variety. In the coloured canaries, Silver is the word used for birds with a white ground colour so that we have Silver Agate, Silver Opal, Silver Brown Satinette, and so on.

SLIPPED CLAW

This is a defective condition of the foot in which the hind toe suffers some form of dislocation, either by slipping forward under the three front toes, or backwards against the shank of the leg. In either case this prevents the bird from gripping its perch properly, and, if it occurs in both feet at the same time, it is most distressing to the sufferer.

It most often happens to young birds during the period after weaning and, if not treated in time, may become a permanent malformation. It may be caused by having perches that are too hard or too large for the young bird's feet, although some fanciers believe it to be an hereditary tendency, or possibly caused by a mineral or vitamin deficiency.

A forward slipped claw is relatively easily dealt with by gently tying back the displaced

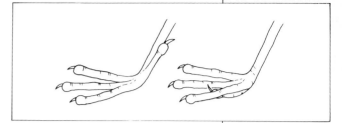

Two ways in which the hind toe may be dislocated

joint against the shank of the leg for a period of about a week or ten days. A small strip of sticking plaster, or something similar, is useful for this purpose but the job needs to be very delicately done. The plaster should not be left on too long otherwise permanent stiffness may result.

The backward dislocation is rather more difficult to deal with and the best treatment is probably to substitute the standard perches with natural springy twigs of about the thickness of a pencil until the bird is seen to be gripping properly once again.

With either method of treatment, some fanciers will first remove all perches for a few days and have a thick layer of sawdust upon the floor. This acts as a soft cushion for the bird's feet, which will have become tender and painful due to strained tendons which are associated with the condition.

SOAKED SEED

In the usual dry seed that is fed to adult birds, the kernel has become tough and hard during the ripening and storing processes. The purpose of soaking the seed is to soften it and thus make it more suitable for nestlings and young stock. (See also *REARING*.)

Some fanciers' seedsmen offer specially prepared mixtures for soaking, or the breeder can make up his own using, in particular, rape, teazle, hemp (if available), canary, sunflower and groats. Any type of seed that the birds are partial to can, in fact be used in a soaking mixture but it is as well to avoid including any linseed which produces a glutinous substance which can make the resulting mixture sticky. Soaking the seeds for 48 hours is quite adequate, changing the water at the halfway stage, and thoroughly washing and draining the seed before giving it to the birds.

Many fanciers also like to offer seed that has been sprouted but the sample will need to be tested first to ensure that it is still live. Not all seeds will germinate, possibly owing to having been kiln dried.

SOFT CONDITION

Fanciers use the term *soft* to describe a bird that is not in vigorous health, whether it be mildly ill or in a more advanced state of sickness. It is the opposite to being in hard condition and may be due to a variety of causes which could be hereditary, respiratory, or digestive in origin. The condition is clearly recognizable as the bird will be listless, dull of eye and loose in feather instead of being its usual bright and lively self. If the problem is respiratory, laboured breathing will be noticed and if digestive there will be wet droppings and possibly some fouling of the vent feathers. If neither of these conditions are in evidence, a weak constitution may be suspected. At all events, steps should be taken to attend to a soft bird otherwise the fancier will have a really sick one on his hands.

A common remedy used by fanciers in former times was to provide the bird with a little bread and milk three or four times a week upon which a few drops of cod liver oil emulsion has been placed, together with a sprinkling of maw seed. At the same time one of the common tonics of the day was added to the water at the rate of about 10 to 15 drops to a drinker of water. Many a bird that was in soft condition improved after a week or so of such treatment but today's fancier is more likely to resort to one of the proprietary bird tonics.

If a bird fails to make a recovery but remains permanently in more or less poor health it is better to take the decision to destroy it. Such birds will never sing, or be of any use for show or prove of any value in the breeding room.

SOFT FOOD

Details of the more commonly used types of soft food are covered under *EGG FOOD* and *REARING*. It was also mentioned that some fanciers often make use of milk sop as well, particularly as a midday feed in place of the morning and evening feeds of egg food. It is all a matter of personal preference but, if used, care must be taken to ensure that the milk sop does not turn sour, which it is liable to do in hot weather. Reference to the previous entry will act as a reminder that bread and milk, sprinkled with cod liver oil and maw seed is often a useful corrective for birds in soft condition.

SOFT MOULT

If the canary casts its feathers other than at the normal moulting season, it is generally referred to as a *soft moult*. It rarely occurs in birds kept by fanciers for breeding and exhibition purposes in an outdoor birdroom but it is not uncommon in the pet bird that is kept in the house. Here the conditions conducive to soft moult often prevail, i.e., draughts, unnaturally high temperatures and fluctuating periods of artificial light.

The casting of the feathers in this case may be continuous, sporadic or only occasional but the continual need to replace lost feathers will obviously place a strain on the bird's general health and overall constitution so that, as a result, it will no longer be in a fit enough condition to entertain its owner with its song.

Once started, a soft moult is often difficult to arrest and an apparent cure may last for a few weeks only to be followed by another bout of feather shedding. As mentioned in *PET CANARY*, attention to those conditions that tend to promote a soft moult is the first step towards effecting a cure. This should be followed by a nourishing diet including a little egg food daily, a small spray of greenfood or seeding weeds according to season, and a tonic in the drinking water.

If a soft moult occurs among breeding stock, they very rarely are fit enough to come into breeding condition for the ensuing season and so the fancier should be prepared to write them off at least until the next season.

SOUTH DUTCH FRILL

In continental Europe this breed is also known by the alternative titles of French Frill and Belgian Frill and these names give a clue to its origin and identity. The frilled feather mutation occurred first in Holland about the year 1800 and birds possessing this characteristic eventually spread to the Southern Netherlands (Belgium) which was the centre of enthusiasm for breeding the *postuurvogel*. Some fanciers incorporated the frilled element with their birds and so produced what was, in effect, a frilled form of the Belgian Canary. Birds of somewhat similar type were also cultivated by fanciers across the border in French Flanders where they were known variously as the Roubaisien or Lillois according to their place of origin.

As with the Belgian Canary itself, this breed was disastrously affected by the two World Wars so that surviving stocks were few and the variety is still far from being numerous.

In type the South Dutch Frill is a combination of the characteristics of its progenitors so that, as stated above, it is virtually a Belgian Canary with frills. Like the North Dutch Frill, only the three basic frills should be in evidence, namely those on the back, breast and flanks. They should be well formed but need not have quite the same voluminous development as in the North Dutch Frill, although perfect symmetry is again of major importance.

The head and neck should be fine and slender like those of the Belgian and should be sleek and free from any frilling. Similarly, the underparts, consisting of the rump, vent, etc., should be smooth feathered and tapering in form.

The South Dutch Frill should be capable of adopting the same typical figure of seven position in the show cage as does the Belgian in order to display both its frills and its posture to the maximum effect when handled by the judge. In this position, the line of the shoulders, back and tail should be perfectly upright and with the head and neck well extended in a forward position, although they need not have the pronounced droop of those of the Belgian but merely be square with the shoulders and back.

Official standard

The standard for this breed as issued by the *C.O.M.* is as follows:
HEAD — Small, slender, serpent-like
BREAST — Small but well filled 'painier'
UNDER BODY — Sleek feathered
FLANKS — Full, bulky, rising well towards shoulder
THIGHS — Smooth feathered
LEGS — Straight
NECK — Elongated, slender, horizontally to the front, smooth feathered
MANTLE — Well furnished, divided by a central longitudinal parting to fall over the shoulders as symmetrically as possible
BACK and TAIL — In a straight line
WINGS — Close to body
PLUMAGE — Soft and undamaged
TAIL — Long and straight
POSITION — forming a figure '7'
SIZE — 17cm

	Points
POSITION AND FORM	10
SIZE	10
PLUMAGE	10
SHOULDERS	10
JABOT	10
FINS	10
LEGS — rigid carriage, thighs feathered	15
TAIL	5
WINGS	5
HEAD	10
GENERAL CONDITION	5
Total	100

SPANGLING

Spangling is the distinguishing feature of the Lizard Canary, the

only variety to be bred entirely for the pattern of its feather markings. The spangling is a series of black, crescent-shaped spots running down the back of the bird in orderly parallel rows and extending well across the back from shoulder to shoulder. These markings are produced by each feather having a black central zone and a lighter coloured edging so that when in place in the normal overlapping sequence like the tiles of a roof the spangled pattern is the result. The more even and regular the spangling, the better it is considered to be and it carries the highest number of points on the official standard scale, 25 out of 100.

SPECIALIST SOCIETIES
These have been mentioned in general terms on several occasions throughout this book so that the reader will already have a fair idea of their purpose. Unlike the local cage bird societies which cater for all kinds of birdkeeping activities, they usually cater for one particular breed of canary only. Many of the present day specialist societies have been in existence for almost a century. Others have sprung up more recently to cater for new breeds or, indeed, for some of the older ones where interest has increased and necessitated further coverage, especially of a regional nature.

The primary aims of any specialist society can be summarized as follows:
1 To maintain, and even improve upon, the standard of the breed they represent.
2 To cater for, and give advice to, fanciers who are interested in those breeds.
3 To publish and issue for general information a *Standard of Excellence* and a *Scale of Points* for judging the breed under their care.
4 To encourage the exhibiting of the breed by granting their patronage to a number of shows each year, holding a club show annually, and by the allocation of special prizes, diplomas,

trophies, etc., to be competed for by its members.
5 To maintain and supervise a panel of competent judges who will be entrusted to officiate at these shows and maintain the Standards as laid down.

A newcomer to the fancy may not wish immediately to join a specialist society but, once he has gained a little experience, and decided which breed he will concentrate upon, he is strongly advised to do so and will certainly benefit from his association with other fanciers with similar interests to his own.

SWEATING
Since birds are unable to sweat, this term is somewhat inaccurate but it is commonly used by fanciers in Britain to indicate an unhealthy condition in a nest of chicks when, instead of being clean and fluffy, they have become damp and messy. It is usually caused by diarrhoea among the nestlings so that the hen is unable to keep the nest clean in the normal way by removal of the faecal sacs.

The most common source of the trouble is food that has become sour. The misfortune can obviously be minimized by proper care and thought in the matter of hygiene, i.e., the removal of all traces of every previous feed when supplying fresh food to the breeding pair, and the regular washing and sterilizing of feeding utensils. If sweating has occured, a clean nest should be supplied, the nestlings gently cleaned up with cotton wool, and a little powdered arrowroot added to the soft food for a day or so until the trouble has disappeared.

SWISS FRILL
The Swiss Frill is another of those European minority breeds that have received the recognition of the *Confederation Ornithologique Mondiale*. There are, in fact, several frilled breeds that differ so little from one another that it is often difficult to tell them apart, even though the published standards may vary in some minor

detail. The Swiss Frill possesses features in common with the South Dutch Frill and the Scotch Fancy (or, perhaps, the Munchener), i.e., the frilling and straight tail of the former, plus the body curvature of the latter.

Official Standard

The Standard of the *C.O.M.* is as follows:

NECK — Long, slender, sleek.
MANTLE — Copious, feathers of the mantle divided by a central parting to fall symmetrically over the shoulders.
TAIL — Long, straight, touching the perch
HEAD — Small, sleek
BEAK — Fine
BREAST FEATHERS — Not too voluminous, symmetrical in the form of a 'painier'
FLANKS — Symmetrical, well raised up
LOWER PARTS — Smooth
LEGS — Long, rigid, thighs covered with small smooth feathers
ATTITUDE — In the form of an ellipse
SIZE — 17cm

	Points
POSITION	10
SIZE	10
PLUMAGE	10
MANTLE	10
JABOT	10
FLANKS	10
HEAD AND NECK	10
LEGS AND THIGHS	15
TAIL	5
WINGS	5
GENERAL CONDITION	5
Total	100

TEAZLE SEED

Teazle (sometimes spelled teasel) has already been mentioned when referring to seed mixtures for canaries, particularly in connection with *CONDITION SEED* and *SOAKED SEED* for rearing. Strangely, it was hardly mentioned in the old standard works on canaries and yet, today, it is a firm favourite with fanciers in spite of its being expensive. Teazle can be grown in the garden but the plants are rather large and a fair number would be needed to produce a reasonable amount of seed. Teazle can also be harvested from the wild, where it tends to grow on wasteland, roadside verges, and so on, especially when damp ditches are present. It should be gathered when almost ripe and hung up in bunches in a dry, airy place until the seed begins to drop when it can be shaken out into a bag.

TECHNICAL MARKINGS

This subject was dealt with under the headings of *CLASSIFICATION, EVEN-MARKED* and *MARKINGS* and definitions were included in the table accompanying the latter entry. Technical markings, as such, are of relatively little importance nowadays although older fanciers, and some specialist societies, still like to make use of the various terms.

These so-called technical markings refer to dark feathers on an otherwise clear bodied bird that occur in three places only, namely the eyes, the secondary flight feathers in the wings, and the outer tail feathers. According to which of these markings a bird may possess, it will be either evenly, or unevenly marked and is designated two-, four-, or six-pointed if evenly marked; or three-, or five-pointed if uneven. (*N.B.* A single one of these marks would usually come within the limits of the definition of a *TICKED* bird. See the following note.)

TICKED

Certain specialist societies have their own standards concerning what constitutes a ticked bird but a widely accepted British definition nowadays is: 'a single area of dark feathers appearing anywhere on the body of an otherwise clear bird and not exceeding a 1p piece in size (20mm), or one wing or tail mark consisting of not more than three adjacent feathers which thus form a single dark mark'.

Norwich Canary with a ticked mark on the back of its head

The latter, of course, might well exceed 20mm in size since the mark would be linear rather than rounded or irregular. As with all forms of marking, there are bound to be some borderline cases over which the judge will naturally exercise discretion.

TOENAILS

As in the case of mammals, a bird's toenails continue to grow throughout its life and therefore will need trimming from time to time. Usually this is only necessary about twice a year and so it does not become a very arduous task. A beginner might understandably be a little nervous at the prospect and may prefer to call upon an experienced fancier to do the job for him. However, armed with a sharp pair of nail scissors, and a degree of determination, he can soon learn to perform the operation quite quickly and efficiently.

The bird should be held in the palm of the hand, with its back to the palm and its head towards the

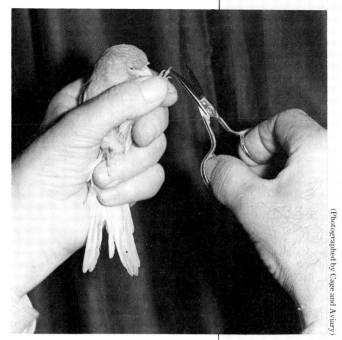

(Photographed by Cage and Aviary)

A different way of trimming a canary's toenails

wrist. Each foot can then be drawn out in turn and held between the thumb and forefinger while the nails are trimmed.

If the nail is held towards the light, the blood vessel can be seen (less easily if the nails are dark). The cut should then be made just beyond the end of the vein so that no bleeding is likely to occur. Once the knack has been acquired, each foot can be dealt with in a matter of seconds.

Nail trimming is always advisable just before the breeding season commences when, even if they are not too long, the sharp tips can be taken off in order to avoid any possible puncturing of the eggs, entanglement in the nesting material, and so on.

TRAINING

This subject was dealt with under *SHOWING*. It must again be emphasized that adequate training is essential if it is intended to exhibit the birds with any expectation of success. Some fanciers may deny the necessity for this and state that, at their first outing the birds will train themselves. While this might possibly be the case with the occasional bird, it should not be made an excuse for laziness.

While undergoing their course of

U V

training, it is important that the show cage drinkers should be in position so that the youngsters will learn where to find their water. At the early shows in the season a bird may be found in a distressed condition for the lack of a drink, until an observant steward notices the trouble and places the drinker inside the cage for a while.

TYPE

Most British breeds and many others from different parts of the world are what are commonly called *type* breeds; that is to say they are essentially bred for their shape or form. This may be coupled with some other attribute such as an impressive, or unusual, stance (e.g. the Yorkshire or the Belgian), a rich colour (the Norwich or the Cinnamon), or some additional adornment of the body (the Crested or the Parisian Frill).

Exceptions are to be found in certain other breeds where type is of secondary importance to the main features such as the markings of the Lizard and the various colours of the Coloured Canaries — also, of course, the song in the case of the Roller.

To the uninitiated, no doubt all the birds of any one breed will look more or less alike, as indeed they should where the breed standard is high. As time goes on, however, the beginner will develop an eye for type. He or she will be able to discern those subtle differences whereby individuals may either excel or fail in certain points which make all the difference between the successful and unsuccessful exhibit.

Whichever breed a newcomer to the fancy decides to take up, he or she should obtain a copy of the Standard and Scale of Points and then endeavour to see as many good living examples of the breed as possible (e.g., at important open shows or by visiting the birdrooms of successful fanciers). In this way the correct type will be fixed in the mind's eye and the breeder will have a yardstick by which to measure his or her own birds and to plan the breeding programmes.

UNDERFLUE

This word is the full form of *FLUE* which was dealt with under that heading. It is the soft, downy part of the feather next to the bird's skin and its colour varies according to that of the web of the feather. In

Feather showing underflue at base of shaft

clear birds it is white, in greens a very dark grey, and in the many colour mutations it may be brown, beige, slate, silver grey and so on. In the interesting, but long extinct variety, the London Fancy Canary, the youngsters in nest feather were just like young Lizards (i.e., dark plumaged Selfs) but, when they moulted out, the web of the feather became clear yellow while the underflue remained dark.

UNFLIGHTED

An unflighted bird is one that is in its first year and has not yet moulted its flight and tail feathers. This it will do at its first full adult moult at the age of just over a year, after which it becomes a flighted or 'overyear' bird (see also *AGE*.)

VARIEGATION

This is a condition in which the canary's plumage pattern is broken up into mainly irregular areas of light and dark feathering. All stages between the Self Green on the one hand and the Clear on the other are, in a sense, variegated but, as we have seen, for the purposes of classification, these have been subdivided into many

different categories such as Ticked, Lightly Variegated, Even Marked, Heavily Variegated, Three Parts Dark, Foul and so on.

VARIETY

In the canary fancy, this term is widely used as interchangeable with the word *breed* although, strictly speaking, it should not be. In the wild, any form of animal, bird or plant life that shows some departure from the definitive type of the species, and is sufficiently distinct and recognizable, is usually designated a *variety*. In the history of the canary, the only departures of this nature have been in the realms of variegation (common to all breeds), pattern (the Lizard and London Fancy) and various colour mutations (in the Coloured Canaries). The distinct breeds as we know them, are purely the creations of man, sometimes aided by mutant forms as, for example, in the case of the Crested and Frilled breeds.

Thus, to be perfectly correct, we have the Norwich Canary, which is a *breed*, and the Ticked, Variegated or Cinnamon forms of the Norwich which are *varieties* of that breed. All of this is, perhaps, purely academic for most fanciers and of no real significance whatsoever, so that they will, no doubt, continue to use the words variety and breed as synonymous terms.

VERY HIGHLY COMMENDED

This is an award, equivalent to fifth in a class, that is made at shows and is usually abbreviated to V.H.C. It is something of a hangover from earlier times and most show authorities now number their awards as First, Second, Third, Fourth, Fifth, Sixth and Seventh. The V.H.C. award does not normally receive any monetary prize.

WEANING

This is always a slightly anxious time for the breeder as it means a complete changeover for the chicks from a state of being entirely dependent upon their parents to that of having to fend for themselves. The vital question always is, 'How soon will they learn to feed themselves?' Most chicks, in fact, normally do so within a few hours of being separated from the old birds but there are always some who seem to be rather backward and do not get the idea very quickly!

It is frequently the case that, so long as the chicks are allowed to remain with their parents, they will make no effort to feed themselves but sit around waiting to be fed. Very often, the longer they are left, the lazier they become and so fanciers usually like to get them away as soon as possible.

The age for doing this will vary according to how well they have been reared, but normally it is at about 21 days old. For a few days prior to this they may well have been out of the nest and, perhaps, even pecking about in an exploratory way at the food provided.

A good time to take the chicks away is in the morning as they will then have the remainder of the day in which to settle in their new quarters and learn to feed themselves. The breeder should not forget to ring them at this time and enter up the ring colours and numbers, and any other relevant details, in the breeding room record book.

A largish feeding board, or tray, measuring about 15cm x 10cm (6in by 4in) is useful at this stage, as the chicks' food can be scattered upon it. Several birds at a time can perch around it in a way that seems to be mutually stimulating as far as learning to feed is concerned. They may not feed, perhaps, for an hour but most will then do so. Any that have obviously not been feeding should be returned to their parents in the late afternoon and another attempt to wean them made the next day.

It will be quite easy to notice the difference, as the chicks that have fed will be quiet and have a contented look about them, whereas the hungry ones will be fluffed up, miserable looking, and periodically uttering plaintive squeaks.

There should be no change in the diet of the newly-weaned birds; the usual egg food, milksop, soaked seed, seeding chickweed, greenstuff, or whatever they have been used to, being given three or four times a day.

Until the chicks are bout six weeks old, some fanciers like to have a floor covering of newspaper in the cages so that it can be changed daily and no stale, or soiled food can possibly be picked up by the youngsters. On the other hand, many fanciers put them straight on to sawdust, sand, etc., according to their normal practice, without them suffering any ill effects.

An alternative method of weaning consists of separating the chicks from their parents in the double breeding cage by means of a wire sliding partition. Chicks and old birds are both given similar food supplies and the idea is that the parents will continue to feed their youngsters through the bars of the slide until they are seen to be picking up food for themselves.

WHITE CANARIES

The two types of White Canaries, the Dominant and the Recessive Whites, have already been dealt with under those headings. Here it is only necessary to add that the two forms should be kept separate and not interbred. If a fancier keeps any of the type breeds of canary, it is probable that all of the Whites he will come across will be of the Dominant variety. On the other hand, if his interest is in Coloured Canaries, they will certainly be Recessive.

WILD CANARY

(see colour feature page 95)

Domesticated canaries originated from wild birds imported from the Canary Islands. It should be noted, that the birds were named after the islands from which they came and not vice versa. The earliest writers, in fact, referred to them as 'Canary birds'.

The canary was first mentioned in writing about the middle of the sixteenth century and so has now been in domestication for almost 450 years. Variations from the wild form, however, were not mentioned until about 300 years ago and were probably not widespread until early in the eighteenth century. Most breeds as we know them, began to emerge from the early 1800s onwards — the Lizard rather earlier (before 1762).

The wild canary is almost identical in appearance to any common crossbred, Self Green, domestic canary; that is to say, about 12.5cm (5in) in length, greyish green on the back, yellowish green underparts and streaked with black on both back and flanks. Wild canaries are still to be found in their original locality and in some other Atlantic islands, such as Madeira and the Azores. For those who may be interested in their distribution and natural history, reference should be made to D. A. Bannerman's *Birds of the Atlantic Islands*.

WILD SEED

Many kinds of wild seeds eaten by native finches are also relished by canaries. Keen fanciers who are in a position to do so will collect from the countryside what they can to supplement their birds' diet. Not only does this effect a useful saving on the seed bills, but also provides various vitamins and minerals that may not be present in the usual hard, dry seed as purchased, which most likely has been kiln dried.

The number of species of plants

whose seed is eaten by birds runs into hundreds. However, since most of today's breeders are more likely to gather seed from the weeds that grow in, and around, gardens the following short list is given: chickweed, shepherd's purse, dandelion, thistle, plantain, sowthistle and various common grasses.

If the fancier does undertake the collecting of wild seeds, care should obviously be taken that no agricultural spraying has recently occurred in the vicinity in order to avoid contamination which could be harmful to the birds.

WING

The wing is naturally an important feature of any bird's anatomy and so it is essential that an exhibition canary should have perfectly formed wings that are properly carried. Fortunately, faults generally are few but, such as there are, they are usually so apparent to the eye that they put a bird out of the running as far as any awards are concerned.

If examined, the feathers of the wing will be seen to consist of the primary and secondary flights, the greater and lesser wing coverts, and the scapulars (the feathers on the shoulders). Although the whole assemblage obviously contributes to the perfect wing shape, irregularities in the flights attract most attention. Such faults can best be described under the headings of *Formation* and *Carriage*.

Formation faults may consist of twisted or displaced flights. In the former, the feathers instead of being flat, have a slight twist to them and so may present an end on, or oblique view to the observer. Fortunately this is fairly rare and may have been caused by dietary inadequacies during rearing, or by plucking while new feathers were still growing. Displaced flights, however, are possibly hereditary defects and so breeding from any such birds should be looked at with circumspection. In this fault, the secondaries cross over the primaries, either above, or below (i.e., the exterior or the inside of the wing) or, in other cases, the primaries themselves cross one another.

The correct carriage of the wing, in almost all breeds, is to have them tightly braced, held close to the body, and with the tips of the flights in line and meeting each other neatly down the middle of the back. Any departures from this clearly constitute faults. At the one extreme, the wings may be held loose and slack, sometimes even drooping below the tail, and on the other hand they may be so braced up as to cross each other at the tips, or even the entire set of flights may cross like a pair of scissors.

However good it may otherwise be, any bird with these wing faults will stand no chance upon the show bench.

WRONG CLASS

A disappointment that may befall the beginner (and sometimes even the more experienced fancier) is to have one, or more, of his or her entries at a show wrong-classed —

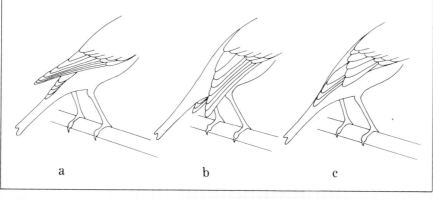

a   b   c

Wing faults:
(a) Crossed flights;
(b) Dropped flights;
(c) Displaced flights

the letters 'W.C.' being written upon the cage label by the judge to indicate this. This can usually be attributed to one of the following reasons:

1 Lack of knowledge — e.g., simply not knowing that a bird is a Yellow or Buff, a Green or a Three-parts dark, and so on. It is to be hoped that the definitions supplied in this book will have helped to eliminate this particular difficulty!

2 Incorrect interpretation of technical terms, show rules, etc. For example, this could be wrongly assuming a bird to be Ticked when, in fact, its marking is large enough to put it in the Marked or Variegated class. Occasionally, too, there are show schedules that have been ambiguously worded so that no fault can really be attributed to the exhibitor. In such a case the judge should either accept the bird as entered, or have it reclassified by the show officials.

3 Genuine mistakes, such as truly believing a bird to be a hen when, in fact, it is a cock. If at judging time it is seen to be singing, the judge will have no option but to wrong class it. In the absence of such obvious proof, the bird might well get away with it, as most judges would not wrong class an exhibit on mere suspicion.

4 Carelessness. This is where even the experienced fancier may err!

When preparing a number of birds for show it is possible, especially if in a hurry, to stick the wrong label on any particular cage. Alternatively, having labelled all of the cages in advance, it is possible then to put the wrong birds into them.

Obviously, with care and correct application of one's knowledge, wrong classing need never occur. However, if it does happen, and the exhibitor does not understand the reason for it, he should not be afraid to ask the judge or, if he is not available, one of the show officials may be able to help. Many judges, in fact, especially in the case of the novice classes, will put a note on the cage label giving their reason for disqualifying the exhibit. This is in order to help the exhibitor to make a correct entry on some future occasion.

There are always some borderline cases where even the judges may be in disagreement and thus it may be possible to have one's bird accepted, and perhaps even win, under one judge and yet have it wrong classed the following week by another adjudicator. Such cases, fortunately, are rare but, if they happen, the exhibitor may decide that the bird in question might better be left at home.

X-CHROMOSOME

Certain characteristics in the canary that are said to be *sex-linked* (e.g., Cinnamon). This means that the gene, or genes, responsible are located on the so-called X-chromosome. A cock bird has two of these, which determine his masculinity, but a hen has only one — the other of the pair being the Y-chromosome.

Because of his two X-chromosomes, therefore, it is possible for a cock to be a carrier of any sex-linked characteristics, e.g., having green (both black and brown melanins) on one chromosome and cinnamon (brown melanin only) on the other. In this case, green being dominant, it is the colour that shows in the plumage of the bird but he can still pass on to some of his progeny the cinnamon that is located on the other chromosome.

A hen, however, because of possessing only the one X-chromosome, must be either a Green or a Cinnamon as she cannot 'carry' any feature that is of a sex-linked nature. The Y-chromosome merely determines her sex and carries no genes for melanin pigmentation. Several other examples of sex-linked mutations have been mentioned elsewhere in this book.

Y

YELLOW

Sufficient has been said about the yellow feather type, and the alternative terms used, for it to be fully understood by the reader of this book. All that need be added here is to advise that, in choosing his breeding pairs, the fancier should select really good examples of the yellow form for mating to their buff partners. That is to say that the Yellows should be of a rich, bright colour with no tendency anywhere to having feathers that may be slightly mealy at the edges.

Unfortunately, in certain breeds, there is a tendency for some Yellows to carry quite a lot of mealing — sometimes to such an extent that it has led to argument as to whether the bird in question was, indeed, a Yellow or a Buff! Clearly, any such birds are to be avoided, however good they otherwise might be, since they will, almost certainly, continue to perpetuate the fault in their progeny. The aim should always be to have birds, whether yellow or buff, that are good examples of their type.

YORKSHIRE

(see colour feature pages 86-87)

In the canary world, the Yorkshire is regarded by many connoisseurs as a supreme example of elegance and refinement, the ultimate achievement of the breeders' art, and it is certainly true that a good Yorkshire will take a lot of beating.

It is not the easiest of birds with which to obtain perfection for here we have a large breed, of some considerable length of body, that must also exhibit the outstanding attributes normally associated with some of the smaller ones, namely suberb style and quality of feather. This, coupled with its confident bearing and upright posture, have given it the old nickname among British fanciers of 'the gentleman of the fancy'.

The Yorkshire is a comparatively late arrival among canary breeds and is generally regarded as having been created during the last quarter of the nineteenth century. The first examples were produced by crossing the common canaries of the British county with the neighbouring Lancashire Plainhead which gave them extra size and length of body; then, to improve their colour and feather quality, the old-fashioned Norwich was introduced. Finally came the idea of refinement by means of a slim and tapering body combined with a good show position, qualities which were obtained from the Belgian Canary.

With all this different blood being blended, the type of those early Yorkshires was somewhat variable but, in 1894, the first official standard for the breed was drawn up and from then on the Yorkshire progressed rapidly and possibly reached the peak of its development in the late 1920s or early 1930s.

Few breeds, however, remain entirely static for long periods of time and more recent trends in breeding have resulted in a bird that differs in some respects from the original standard of the breed. This is particularly noticeable in such features as the fuller, bolder head and shoulders which give to the bird what is called by fanciers *top end*, and so the modern standard has been amended accordingly.

The Yorkshire is now the only popular variety among those breeds of canary known as birds of position that include the Belgian and Scotch Fancy. It has an alert and graceful poise of the body in the show cage which is so important a feature that one quarter of the points are allotted for it. This posture should be erect and confident with never any inclination to crouch nor to stand at a low angle across the perch.

After the full top end of head and

shoulders the body should taper away gradually towards the tail in a prolonged wedge shape with no excess of feather at the waist or thighs to spoil the line. In this breed the tail, instead of being an exact extension of the line of the body, should be carried with just a perceptible lift to it but not so pronounced as to spoil the harmony of the bird's outline and balance.

This is a fine breed which, although not normally regarded as beginner's material, could very well provide the right outlet for anyone who wanted something a little out of the ordinary to start with.

Official standard
The official standard and scale of points that has been agreed to by all Yorkshire specialist societies is as follows:

Points

HEAD — Full, round and cleanly defined. Back skull deep and carried back in line with rise of shoulders. Eye as near centre of head as possible. Shoulders proportionately broad, rounded and carried well up to and gradually merging into head. Breast full and deep, corresponding in width and rise to shoulders and carried up full to base of beak which should be neat and fine   20

BODY — Well rounded and gradually tapering throughout to tail   10

POSITION — Attitude erect with fearless carriage, legs long without being stilty, and slight lift behind   25

FEATHER — Close, short and tight. Wings proportionately long and evenly carried down the centre of the back and firmly set on a compact and closely folded tail   25

SIZE — Length approximately 6¾in with corresponding symmetrical proportions   10

CONDITION — Health, cleanliness and sound feather, colour pure and level   10

Total 100

The Yorkshire specialist societies have a standard for markings which often differs in certain respects from those in more general use. The Yorkshire fancier, therefore, will need to familiarize himself with these when entering his birds for any show which is held under the auspices of a Yorkshire specialist society.

YOUNG STOCK SHOWS
Some of the local cage bird societies run a young stock show for the benefit of their members at which birds of the current year may be exhibited. Some of these shows are held in early summer, in which case most young birds will still be in their nest feathers. If held later on, the early hatched birds might well be through their first moult.

Young stock shows are not always well supported. Many fanciers feel that it is too early to push their young birds out to a show and so, to increase the overall entries, classes are often provided for adult birds as well. Thus, the local young stock show might provide the beginner with his first experience of showing his birds as the atmosphere is usually informal and not too highly competitive.

144